rewired Life

*a journey to untangle
chronic pain and endometriosis*

AUDREY MICHEL

BALBOA
PRESS

A DIVISION OF HAY HOUSE

Balboa Press books may be ordered through booksellers or by contacting:

Balboa Press
A Division of Hay House
1663 Liberty Drive
Bloomington, IN 47403
www.balboapress.com
1 (877) 407-4847

Because of the dynamic nature of the Internet, any web addresses or
links contained in this book may have changed since publication and
may no longer be valid. The views expressed in this work are solely those
of the author and do not necessarily reflect the views of the publisher,
and the publisher hereby disclaims any responsibility for them.

The author of this book does not dispense medical advice or prescribe the use
of any technique as a form of treatment for physical, emotional, or medical
problems without the advice of a physician, either directly or indirectly. The
intent of the author is only to offer information of a general nature to help you
in your quest for emotional and spiritual well-being. In the event you use any
of the information in this book for yourself, which is your constitutional right,
the author and the publisher assume no responsibility for your actions.

Any people depicted in stock imagery provided by Thinkstock are models,
and such images are being used for illustrative purposes only.
Certain stock imagery © Thinkstock.

Print information available on the last page.

ISBN: 978-1-5043-3884-4 (sc)
ISBN: 978-1-5043-3886-8 (hc)
ISBN: 978-1-5043-3885-1 (e)

Library of Congress Control Number: 2015913054

Balboa Press rev. date: 10/21/2015

contents

introduction

Everybody has something to deal with: a mountain to climb, a hole to dig out of, a ravine to cross, or a demon to conquer. Mine were called chronic pain and endometriosis.

In 1995 at age 14, I was diagnosed with endometriosis, a painful reproductive disease that occurs when cells lining the uterus grow outside the uterus and into other areas of the abdomen and body. The disease can cause pain, irregular bleeding, infertility, and myriad other symptomatic issues. According to Endometriosis.org an estimated 176 million women and girls, or approximately 1 in 10, are affected by endometriosis to varying degrees worldwide.[1] After being diagnosed, I spent the next decade as a permanent fixture in doctors' offices enduring surgeries, hormone treatments, pain medication, muscle relaxers, mood stabilizers, and various therapies to help with the excruciating amount of physical pain. The height of pain was between the years of 2007 and 2009.

For two weeks out of the month, during menstruation and ovulation, you could find me in bed or on the sofa, sporting the latest fashion in hooded sweatshirts and yoga pants, snuggling with my cats. It sucked not to get out of bed for days, to have taken the maximum dosage of pain pills before noon, and to feel so drugged up and foggy that I couldn't recall 50 percent of the conversation

---

[1] Facts about endometriosis, http://endometriosis.org/resources/articles/facts-about-endometriosis/

I'd just held. Since I had endured chronic pain for so long, a pain level of 6 was a good day.

I know now that it is possible to live free of chronic pain and free of the symptoms of endometriosis. It is possible to feel no pain and be fully functioning during every day of menstruation and ovulation. But it took almost two decades to discover the possibilities. It took almost two decades to discover my power.

In January 2009, I snapped. I not only hit rock bottom, but I also kept digging. It wasn't until my perspective shifted that I began a journey to really heal my body and spirit. I embraced a holistic lifestyle of clean eating, acupuncture, chiropractic, massage, kinesiology, yoga, and meditation. I thought I knew my body. I thought I knew how to take care of myself. But all I knew was pain.

I started listening to my whole body, mind, and spirit. Now I view my body as a message board that displays what is going on in my spirit and psyche. Endometriosis and chronic pain clearly affected my physical body, and, as years went on, layer upon layer of pain affected my emotional body more than I ever knew. Although the emotional body can be difficult to comprehend, the physical body isn't. I like to imagine the emotional body as an exact copy of the physical body, just as an amoebic overlay. I ignored my emotional body for far too long. I treated it like some ugly stepsister that I kept shoving into the corner. When it did work up the courage to say something, I looked at it like an imbecile - worthless, annoying, and stupid. I bullied that part of myself, beating up my emotional body, leaving it shaking and crying, huddled in the corner with fear.

At the same time, my physical body was riddled with pain, and I gave it my full attention. So when specialists told me they could do nothing more, that moment sparked a downward spiral. What do you do when everything you've ever known to do no longer works? When the system you've put all of your hopes into for recovery no longer has answers? I chased more doctors and more specialists down the rabbit hole of more tests and more pills.

At my darkest hour, my beaten, emotional body stood up from

the corner and asked, "Are you going to listen to me now? I'm the one hurting and broken. I need love and attention. I know so much, and there is so much I have to tell you."

My endometriosis story starts the day my endometriosis ended. My story starts the day of my fourth laparoscopy surgery as my surgeon told my husband and I there was no visible sign of endometriosis. My endometriosis story starts the day my specialist told me, "There is nothing more I can do for you." My endometriosis story starts the day I embraced my demons and embraced that endometriosis is in my heart, in my head, in my spirit, and in every cell of my body. Endometriosis hurt every part of my being. Endometriosis took me away from me. I didn't love me. I didn't love my body. I didn't love living my life.

Now I know my endometriosis story has power. My story picks up where the doctors left off, where I discovered and began embracing myself. I am the only one with the power to shower myself with the unconditional love needed to dig out of the corner this disease put me in.

Through it all, I reclaimed the connection to my body, what it needs, and the right to express and honor that, especially in the presence of doubt and negativity. I continue to shrink the disconnection between my head and my heart, reconnecting to my whole self. I now trust my internal compass and wisdom.

Rewired Life is my story about overcoming physical pain and disease. *Rewired Life* is also about acknowledging, accepting, and loving all parts of myself. It is my story of how I healed my physical, emotional, *and* spiritual body.

Everyone is worthy and deserving of health and well-being. I don't know your story or what your mountain looks like, but what I do know is that we all have our own journeys. We have to discover what course of action fits our individual needs. And when we let go of fear, resentment, and negativity, we move from darkness into light.

chapter 1

faster, stronger, better

Love yourself first and everything else falls into line.
—Lucille Ball

On days when chronic pain reared its ugly head, the cold linoleum of the kitchen floor was the most comforting. Most days of menstruation and ovulation felt like a shit-storm of awfulness. Menstruation was painful and exhausting, and ovulation caused stabbing back pain. I would have given anything to be anywhere but where I was. I dreamt of the day when the pain and endometriosis would be gone: My husband and I would go on an awesome vacation to celebrate—I couldn't wait for that day.

For twelve years, I used Western medicine to help with chronic pain and endometriosis, relying on one drug or another to get through the day. Looking back now, I know I never felt well. There were times when I felt awful, and there were times when I felt better, but I never felt healthy. At the worst of it, I'd wake up to a solid dose of pain pills. Eight hours of sleep equaled eight hours without prescription pain meds. Let me tell you, the growly bear angrily waking from its slumber was not pleasant. As I woke up, I needed the next dose, and it wasn't safe to get between me and those pills. Actually, it wasn't even safe to talk to me for at least an hour. I needed a swift kick in the ass—called Darvocet—to inch my way toward being awake.

As I peeled my body out of bed, gathered myself, made it to work, or whatever else was necessary for the day, I appeared to be a functioning human being. But I was on autopilot. Most of my actions were a blur. I probably should not have been driving, and I definitely needed to stop for a white chocolate mocha to jolt me into reality. Mornings mostly consisted of waiting for pain relievers to kick in and trying to remember what I was supposed to be doing. By noon, I'd have two more doses of pain pills—*let's just call that lunch because I wasn't hungry anyway.*

For the afternoon, I'd hit up more meds, maybe a muscle relaxer and some Prozac as I felt the irritation of the day intensifying. Late afternoon required a nap. Between exhaustion as a drug side effect and the exhaustion of suppressing pain and body tension, I was constantly running on empty. All I wanted was to flop on the sofa like a sack of potatoes. Don't even talk to me about doing anything past late afternoon; I was done! I used all my energy reserves to merely exist.

After waking up from my nap, I'd try to eat dinner, but nothing ever tasted good. By night, it was time for sleeping pills. Over-the-counter sleeping pills seemed to do the trick. I was glad not to be on prescription sleeping pills, too—all I needed was another addictive drug on the list. Doctors were already rotating my pain pills from the stand-by Darvocet to Bextra, Percocet, Naproxen, and Propoxyphene to prevent addiction. For really bad days, Vicodin or Meperidine would knock me out. I'd pop a couple of those bad boys and pass out. Sleeping equaled forgetting. I welcomed anything that kept pain from my consciousness.

My daily hormone regimen consisted of one of the first and stronger birth control pills on the market. I needed birth control to regulate timing, heaviness, PMS, and cramping from my period. Modern products contain fewer hormones since the average woman doesn't need high dosages. However, those things were like sugar pills to me; they never even affected the timing or symptoms of my period. Miserable. Without all the medication, my body wouldn't be capable of functioning properly—how else would it regulate itself? I had to have medicine. There was no other way.

By late 2007, the pain was in full force once again. History told me it was time for another surgery to eliminate new endometriosis growth and accumulated scar tissue. This would be my fourth laparoscopy. I called my doctor, said, "It's time," and scheduled the surgery and time off work for this regular maintenance. I remember strolling into the hospital thinking, *No big deal. This will be like the last one. Get rid of endometriosis tissue and scar tissue and buy myself a few years of reduced pain.*

Doctors found trace amounts of scar tissue, which they cleaned up, but no visible signs of endometriosis tissue. Typically, laparoscopy surgeries bought me three to five years of relief. My husband, Aaron, recalls viewing the post-surgery images that showed clean, healthy tissue. We should have been ecstatic. The endometriosis tissue was gone! Wasn't that supposed to be my dream? Instead, Aaron was worried about my reaction. We both had been sure surgery was going to ease the pain. Not this time. With only trace amounts of scar tissue removed, where was the pain coming from? I thought, *What am I supposed to do now?* It didn't make any sense.

For years I had kept my OB-GYN in Omaha, Nebraska. No matter where I lived, I always returned home to see that doctor. He'd been taking care of me since I was a teenager. He knew me. I knew him. It was comfortable. If pain was building, I'd return home for surgery, recover for a few days, head back to wherever I was living, and get back to life.

This time was different. After the surgery, I returned to Denver. I was still in pain and supposedly free from endometriosis tissue. My doctor had done all he could do from eight hours away. Not a single physician in Denver knew my name. Over the next few months, I was stuck in a desperate, frantic cycle to find a doctor to fix me.

I remember one particularly awful day in early 2008. In pain and crying, I'd taken more pills than a 120-pound person ever should. Aaron was traveling for work, and my mom could only comfort me over the phone. My doctor in Nebraska didn't know why I hurt so badly and had nothing more to offer than telling me, "No more pain pills." And he didn't know any OB-GYNs in Denver to call in a favor.

I was alone. I was scared. I was desperate. But this time desperate didn't mean resigned. It lit a fire under my ass. I researched every gynecologist in the city, picked out the perfect one, and made a phone call.

"We aren't accepting new patients at this time." *Ugh—what the hell! Okay, my second choice physician would have to work.* I called that office only to hear that new patient appointments were six to eight weeks out. *OMG! I don't have eight weeks. I don't have eight days. I don't even want to think about feeling this way for eight more hours!* I contemplated going to the emergency room, but they'd only do what they usually do—give me more pain meds. I'd already taken too many.

I called every gynecologist office within my insurance network and said yes to every waiting list. I called every hospital and got on their clinic waiting lists. I called my girlfriends for referrals. I even made Aaron ask the ladies at his office for referrals.

And then I passed out from exhaustion—and maybe a drug-induced coma.

I awoke to my phone ringing. Half asleep, I answered.

"Hello, is this Audrey?"

"Yeah," I said, barely conscious.

"This is blah-blah-blah from the office of blah, I have you on our waiting list."

My eyes shot open.

She continued, "You aren't at the top of my list, but I feel like you could use some help."

I doubt anything intelligible came out of my mouth, and if it did I'm sure she couldn't understand it through my tears. She gave me an appointment for the next day.

I cried. And then I collapsed back onto my bed.

———•

After finding an OB-GYN in Denver to see me, the next few weeks filled up with appointments, tests, and more tests to figure out why I was in so much pain. The new OB-GYN passed me along to an endometriosis specialist who came highly recommended and, at the time, seemed to be exactly what I needed. After an elongated discussion, he suggested Lupron shots, a series of injections that manipulate hormones and put women through medically induced menopause. The drug starves endometriosis cells of their life-blood: estrogen. The thought is that, without estrogen, the endometriosis tissue will not grow, and, best case scenario, the endometriosis cells shrink, leaving patients with less pain. The idea behind using Lupron at this point was that there must have been endometriosis tissue that the previous surgeon might have missed.

Once the specialist discovered this would be my third round of Lupron, he ordered a bone density test.

For real? My mind went into overload. *I'm 27!* I thought to myself, *Bone density test? Not okay. I knew the hormone treatments were harsh—but osteoporosis?* It turns out that one of the side effects of this medically forced menopause, as many women experience with actual menopause, is bone density loss and early onset osteoporosis.

During previous rounds of Lupron, I remember being aware of potential side effects, hot flashes, mood swings, etc. I was never too concerned about them; side effects were just another part of treating endometriosis. I thought the drug was helping me in the long run by stunting the growth of endometriosis, so I could overlook side effects. But this looming round of hormone treatments felt different.

It was my husband who spoke up. He told me he always hated what Lupron did to me and asked, "Do you know what that stuff looks like? A toxic, hot pink, magenta, nuclear concoction. It's got to be terrible for your body!" Never before had I really considered the effect on my overall health. I could deal with hot flashes and mood swings. But osteoporosis?

No.

This time Lupron didn't feel right. Now, thirteen years after my diagnosis, for the first time I was saying *no* to treatments that didn't make sense for me.

Previously, I would have said that Lupron and other medical treatments were successful. But could I really call it success if I was living déjà-vu for the fourth time? I was frustrated to hear the only option was to continue down the same treatment path.

Surviving the first thirteen years of the disease was a combination of numbing any feeling with Western medicine's latest and greatest pain relief method, some crazy hormone concoction, and pretending I was fine. This all had seemed to work—but before I knew it, my daily regimen of medicine added up to well over a dozen pills. And I was taking medicine to deal with the side effects of other medicines. I no longer knew the difference between my own feelings or how one particular drug or another made me feel. I was in a constant fog, completely disconnected from myself, and completely unaware of that fact.

I was doing everything I knew to do—and not improving. I was at a dead end and feeling helpless. Actually, I was getting worse. The only thing I knew to do was to sleep. When I was sleeping, I couldn't feel. I checked out. When I was awake, I dropped into even more physical and emotional pain. I lost hope, and depression took control of my life. I did my best to put one foot in front of the other, put on a pretty face, and "get on with life." That is what I was supposed to do, right?

If doctors couldn't figure out why I was in so much pain, how much worse could it get? I was scared to know what the future would be like without medication. Think about it, if the pain level was around an 8 out of 10 with pain medication, could I imagine life without them? Pain could be at 50! What choice did I have? The potential to experience worse pain kept me tied to ever-expanding prescriptions. My belief that medications must be making me better compounded my fear of how bad it would be without them.

It was hard to wrap my brain around this: I was out of options. This was as good as it was going to get. What did this even mean? Looking back now, I have so many questions for myself. I was stuck in pain because I was scared of being well? Scared of what unmedicated pain might look like? Scared of not having pain as an excuse? Scared of not having pain tolerance as a badge of honor? Scared to know what was underneath all the pain? I can't help but wonder, *What was this fear doing to me psychologically?* How did this inability to see beyond medications affect my whole health?

How many times in your life have you felt stuck? Even more important, how many times have you been stuck and not even known?

My fear played a dangerous role in my declining health. I placed my need to be well in the hands of people who barely knew me– people who authentically wanted to help but only knew what my medical chart told them: long history of endometriosis and chronic pain. Doctors did what they were trained to do, and for that I am grateful. But it was time for me to take control of my health and my body and do what was best for me. I seriously had no idea what the hell that looked like, but I finally asked, "What else is possible? What else can I be doing?" I didn't realize it at the time, but my awareness and priorities were finally shifting.

For years I believed that my only option to get better was to do what the doctor said. I'm not sure if it was because I was a teenager when I was diagnosed or because I was from a small town where alternative medicine and second opinions were not available, but I had always followed the doctor's orders. No questions asked.

When none of the experts have answers, what are we supposed to do? What happens when we've done prescribed treatments and the pain is the same or even worse? These questions and situations can feel impossible.

Are there decisions being made for you when it comes to your health? Decisions that leave you feeling powerless? Are there treatments you are currently following that you don't feel good about?

For me, it was a slow transition to ask, "What else is available?" After saying no to Lupron, light bulbs began to turn on, and the walls blocking my vision slowly began fall like dominoes. I realized that conventional ways of thinking and conventional medical treatments no longer fit me.

Now I know abundant possibilities for improving health and wellness are alive within me and alive in the world. Becoming open to the idea that there was more to know sent a powerful message to my body, mind, and spirit. Being open to exploring what my body needs created curiosity and a need for exploration.

Wouldn't it be great if we were able to hear the messages our bodies are sending sooner? We can! I started the journey to understand what triggers me physically, emotionally, and mentally—this helps me see and hear when my body needs a change. For me the shift started with my first *no* and grew as I figured out how and why my body reacts in different situations.

chapter 2

trauma and the great disconnection

The feeling of being disconnected from ourselves is often the most painful. We lose grounding. We lose our authenticity. The reason this is so painful is because our authenticity is the very foundation from which all meaningful change occurs.
—Brené Brown, I Thought It Was Just Me (but It Isn't)

iving with physical pain and emotional trauma is like looking through a zoom lens of a camera– zoomed in so close you can only see the details. My only concern at the peak of physical pain was surviving day to day. I couldn't see my future as any different than the current moment. The disease was at the forefront of my life, and it had taken over. Pain sucked any and all real joy out of me. I thought if I focused all my attention on making the pain go away, I could live a normal life. But all I could see was endometriosis and chronic pain. On one hand, I pretended to be fine and continued everyday life. On the other hand, I was depressed and tired of being tired.

I was also really tired of telling my tale, regurgitating my "endo stats," and continually answering repeated questions. What's your pain level? When was your last cycle? Did pain coincide with your cycle? Where was the pain located? Would you describe it as radiating, stabbing, throbbing, or continuous? How are you sleeping? What pills did you take on what day?

Once I finished telling nurses about every bowel movement,

every detail of my last period, and reviewing mood swings to the point of bringing on another one, I still had to talk to the doctor. I never understood why the nurse and the doctor never spoke to each other prior to walking into my exam room. Wouldn't it be more efficient to review my answers? *But no, no problem. I'll answer the same questions for a second time in the last fifteen minutes. I mean, I love talking about how wonderful and fabulous I've been feeling. Remember those mood swings we were talking about? . . .Let's do talk about how shitty things have been lately.*

One doctor after another, this nurse after that nurse—I continually relived the story of how broken my body had become. And all it did was reinforce how stuck I was in the situation, perpetuate the trauma, and force the situation back into my consciousness.

Usually, my answer sounded like this, "Pain level of 10. I hurt all the time. I sleep all the time. And I continually take pills." I honestly didn't want to dig deeper into how I was truly feeling. How would it help anyway? I'd recounted my issues to dozens of healthcare professionals and still felt like hell. What more was there to know? The thought of really sitting with the pain, contemplating how it was affecting my daily life, and paying attention to it throb through my core and into my limbs made me depressed and angry. Couldn't we just stop talking about it? The faster we could talk through how shitty I felt, the better.

Remembering didn't make me happy. Nothing made me feel better. I stopped noticing the nuances from one day to the next. What was the point?

———•———

After my first surgery in early 1996, the next step to continue reducing endometriosis cells was hormone treatments. That was when I received my first Lupron prescription. As a fourteen-year-old girl, I went through menopause. I got it all: the mood swings, the hot flashes, and the night sweats. The eight-month treatment was nothing less than a hormonal disaster. I was a ticking time bomb. I skipped from the socially awkward and confusing experience of getting my period to the dreadful later-in-life changes of menopause.

My grandmother and I would swap stories. The clothes go on; the clothes come off. "I'm freezing; I'm sweating." "Is anyone else hot? OMG, turn the heater off!" We'd compare hormone supplements: "Do you like the pills or the cream?"

Even though my grandma and I got a good laugh out of our unlikely shared experience, whom was I supposed to talk to my own age? Who was talking about taking birth control pills in the eighth grade? What friend of mine was seeing an OB-GYN on a bimonthly basis? Who was talking about menopause? I couldn't talk about my period with other girls my age; I had nothing in common with them. "What's menopause? That's weird." I hated it.

Emotionally traumatizing? Probably.

I missed any joyful experiences of becoming a woman and never knew my reproductive organs could provide something other than pain, dysfunction, and ongoing hormonal storms. I resented being a woman. All of the trauma made me hate my body, and I felt trapped. Can you begin to imagine how much mental and emotional work I had to do around accepting myself as a woman later in life?

Between the hormone treatments and pain pills, I was a mess of side effects and emotions. I could be happy, or I could be sad, depressed, or angry. I just woke up and spun the Roulette Wheel of Emotions. No one ever knew which emotion was going to show up on any given day or any given moment. And I sure didn't understand the varying emotions and mood swings. My perception was *I'm fine. Everyone else is crazy and hard to get along with. What's your problem?!*

To add to the drama, I couldn't remember conversations hour to hour. I didn't remember that yesterday you asked how I was feeling and I vomited an explosion of curse words upon you—now today you didn't ask how I am doing, and I am sad, depressed, and crying—*don't you care?* Those around me would insist we'd talked about a particular topic, and I was convinced we had not. Looking back, portions of my life just do not exist. They were erased, as if they never happened—which was a blessing for some situations and a curse for others.

———

Endometriosis and chronic pain sufferers have a few things working against us. First, chronic pain is hard for the average person to relate to, whereas being in acute physical pain is more socially acceptable. If you break your leg, people go out of their way to be helpful. With chronic pain, however, people are sympathetic for all of forty-five minutes and then they are over it. It's not that others don't care; it's just hard to visibly see chronic pain. And without a visible reminder, people forget. Second, endometriosis is a *woman's problem*. Don't you love that? Even if I was experiencing awful pain, it was still just "cramps."

One day in eighth grade, I went to the nurse's office wanting to go home. "I have my period, and it hurts really bad. I need to go home," I said.

The nurse laughed, handed me some Tylenol, and told me, "Those are cramps, Honey. We all get those. You can go back to class."

I was embarrassed and wanted to cry. I left the nurse's office but didn't go back to class. I knew I had an ally in the principal's office, Jeanie. Jeanie let me call my mom and go home.

For most teenagers, self-awareness is low to begin with. Add chronic pain, heavy medication, and severe hormone imbalances, and it was hard to understand what was a side effect and what was real. I struggled to understand myself. Was I an unstable mix of emotions or was instability a side effect? As I look back, it's as if my body, mind, and spirit were in fight-or-flight mode at all times. I couldn't see outside of myself.

People often ask me how I was able to deal with endometriosis and chronic pain at such a young age. I simply didn't know anything different. I didn't have previous experiences to compare. From the time my cycle started, I had extremely painful menstruation, ovulation, and PMS. It's like asking a person born blind what it is like not to see.

As years went on, I no longer had to deal with hardened school nurses. Now shame and embarrassment came in the form of bosses and coworkers. Try telling unsympathetic coworkers that your uterus hurts. I had one female coworker tell me I was lazy because cramps weren't sick-day excuses, and I should have to take a vacation day to stay at home and watch movies. Another female coworker tried to empathize with me, commenting that she gets the "worst" cramps, and proceeded to ask if I'd ever tried Midol. "That stuff is magic!" she said.

Over-the-counter meds, how cute. I could make a fortune on the streets with the pills required to cut through pain, I thought to myself.

At one point, a male boss did his best to be helpful and said, "Oh yeah, I know endometriosis. I think my wife had that. But it went away after having kids. You're married, aren't you? You should start having kids." At 25 I was thinking, *Yeah right, be right on that!*

Over the years I got smarter and, instead of leading with cramps, I just called it pain and mentioned all the pills I was taking. Telling my boss it took several prescription pain pills to get out of bed and that I legally shouldn't be driving was easier than, "No really my cramps are worse than other women's." I learned what words to use and which ones *not* to use.

I also excelled at the art of skimming over my own feelings in order to fit in. My need to avoid talking about endometriosis trumped any attempt to let my feelings or needs be heard. I could understand that I was hurting and that I was accumulating physically traumatic events. That was clear. My inability to acknowledge and express feelings allowed mental and emotional issues to mount unaddressed. And one area where I suppressed my voice and my feelings without knowing it was the doctors' offices.

The endometriosis diagnosis "required" repeated pelvic exams that began as an early teenager to make sure my uterus and ovaries were healthy and to make sure I wasn't developing cysts. It was always painful, and I endured it because I believed it was best to hold it together, to be strong. It took all my strength not to cry during the appointment. Having your cervix examined is uncomfortable for any woman (or so I've been told), but for me, it would take days to recover from the extreme physical pain of a pelvic exam.

At the time, I understood the procedure as a necessary part of the diagnosis and obligatory for the doctor to understand the condition of my organs. I thought I didn't have a choice. If I wanted to get better, I had to do what the doctor needed. And every time I went to the doctor for anything endometriosis related, they needed to do a pelvic exam. Each time I placed no value on my own feelings. Each time I didn't feel heard; each time I felt like the doctors viewed me as broken. I really wanted to pretend like it wasn't happening. Yet each time another layer of trauma built up inside me.

Doctor appointments were confusing. I mean, women and girls around the world go to the OB-GYN all the time, so why did it suck so badly for me? I felt like I was the only one leaving in tears, embarrassed, and ashamed.

Anxiety and fear built appointment after appointment. It never occurred to me to ask if the exams were necessary, to mention that they were extremely painful, or to ask if there was another way. I just kept my feelings to myself and did what was expected of me.

All of my doctors were male. All of them were trying to fix me. All of them had strong opinions about what I should do next. Not one of them asked what I wanted.

The pattern of ignoring my feelings and putting others' opinions ahead of my own created disconnection between my head and my heart. Repeatedly, my emotional needs were shut down and invalidated. I continually sent messages to my psyche that whatever it had to say was unnecessary, unwanted, and not worth mentioning. I had no voice. My ability to vocalize my needs was lost, and my ability to feel in control of my own body and my own health was gone.

It's as though with each visit I'd put my negative experiences and trauma in a jar and hid it from myself. I found the perfect hiding spot deep down in my psyche. I didn't know that this pattern was laying groundwork for unexpected breakdowns, trauma, dysfunctional relationships, and an unbalanced lifestyle. One day all the emotional hurt would come pouring out of me, begging for the attention it never received.

I was blindly hopping and skipping about, not looking at my internal compass. The less I listened to internal wisdom, the less it spoke up. After a while, the gap between my head and my heart widened. I completely disconnected from my sense of self. I would do anything to make the pain go away, and, appointment after appointment, I gave away my power and voice. Rage and fury built inside me. I didn't know it at the time, but my internal wisdom had something to communicate and was determined that I hear it. The only way my body could get me to listen to what it had to say, reconnecting my head and heart, was to stage an intervention.

———

I never considered myself as being unstable or battling mental issues or depression. I always thought of myself as a normal person who had this other "thing" to deal with from time to time. I never viewed endometriosis as affecting my relationships, my education, my career, or me as a person. Nor did I understand that the treatment of the disease was causing emotional trauma. All I understood was that my *body* hurt. If the physical pain went away, I thought I would be so much better off. I would be happy. But that's not what happened. Emotional pain built in my subconscious. It was like gremlins established residency, grew a colony, and prepared for a hostile takeover of my psyche at an unknown date in the future.

I always thought trauma was some big thing other people experienced. Like post-traumatic stress disorder for soldiers returning from war, a woman being brutally raped, or maybe a bad car accident leaving someone with physical handicaps. Other people experience trauma. Not me. Nothing bad ever happened to me. I'm from a loving home in a middle-class, Midwestern town. I had nothing to complain about. I could be worse, so I must be fine. I unknowingly and ignorantly thought if I sucked it up and didn't talk about hurt feelings, then the stress and trauma would just go away.

Let me tell you, it doesn't go away. Stress, negativity, and trauma fester inside like a bad infection, manifesting as pain, disease, and dysfunction. The longer stress and trauma are left untouched, the more serious and life-threatening the eventual outcome can be.

If I had to go back and relive past painful events now that my hormones and emotions are stable, I would have a different experience. At the time, I couldn't comprehend the quality of life that was taken from me. I couldn't comprehend how depressing it was to lay in bed for days or to have lost the desire to get out of bed. I chose to numb pain with pills, and as I dulled the pain, I dulled *all* feeling. I didn't realize I was numbing the highs *and* the lows. I welcomed a break from pain but later understood how numbing also robbed me of joy and pleasure. You don't know what you don't know. And I didn't know I could experience pain-free menstrual cycles or that life could be so much more easy and enjoyable.

chapter 3

perfect pretender

Be yourself; everyone else is taken.
—Oscar Wilde

did my best to separate my health from the rest of my life. The longer the disease went on, the more disconnected the two became until I thought the two had nothing to do with each other. It's like I stuffed all the awful experiences in a closet and ignored them. At first the closet doors shut, but before long so much crap accumulated in the closet that I needed one hand to hold the door shut. Then I needed both hands. Then both hands and a foot, which meant I only had one leg to hold up the rest of my life. I became skilled at putting on a pretty face. I didn't want anyone to be able to tell I wasn't feeling well. I didn't care if anyone intellectually knew I had an illness, but I did care if anyone could physically see that I was in pain. I used every ounce of energy to hide how I felt from others—and unknowingly from myself. I compartmentalized my health, and it seemed to work. But I was only fooling myself.

Pouring my energy into sports and activities became my escape. If I could be just like everyone else, then I must not be sick. It must not be that bad. Pushing myself physically not only proved I was fine, but it also helped me *feel*. It's true, exercise produces endorphins that improve mental and physical health, but for me it was more than that. The rush of competition and testing my physical limits pushed endometriosis and pain to the back of my mind. I could *feel* my body despite all the pain pills and hormones. I could feel something other than the pain and medicated fog I was used to. I felt connected to myself and like I was connected to others and part of something bigger. I felt in control. I didn't care how exhausted endometriosis or chronic pain made me, I found energy for sports. As an athlete I paid attention to my body. I was meticulous about monitoring caloric intake, heart rate, hydration, and a training schedule. I cared for my body because I could see a direct correlation between care and performance.

Although experiencing physical pain and symptoms of endometriosis, I was psychologically convinced that being physically and socially active meant I was fine and, therefore, must be conventionally healthy. I never thought of myself as being sick. I believed that people who are sick couldn't get out of bed. Sick people don't go out with friends, swim hundreds of laps a week, or run a successful business. Looking back, I see how it made sense. I wanted a break from the reality of painful menstrual cycles and exhausting back pain, so I clung to anything that helped me forget. It was my way to survive.

———

As a child, I had trained as a competitive gymnast, so the idea of pouring all my energy into sports came naturally. After gymnastics, I turned my focus to high school sports. I ran track and played softball. I was on the swim team and high school dance team. If I could be a good athlete even through all the pain, it was like earning an extra gold star. Keeping my mind and body busy helped me cope with pain and fit in. The more the pattern to hide the pain and disease repeated itself, the less I noticed what was happening inside my body. Obsessing over one challenging activity or another became a place of comfort. I knew how to forget pain in those situations, and I knew who I was.

This strategy worked successfully through high school, college, my career as a commercial interior designer, and my photography business. I would work my ass off then come home and crash. Being the best I could be at whatever I set my mind to defined me. Makes sense, doesn't it?

In reality, overachieving was covering up the disease that was slowly eating away at me physically and psychologically. I rationalized my habits since they helped me deal with chronic pain, emotional stress, and isolation caused by endometriosis. Coping mechanisms are normal in dealing with ongoing illness—but that doesn't mean they are helpful. This need to overachieve and drain myself physically finally caught up with me.

In early 2008, I fell in love with cycling. What started with borrowing a road bike to ride an MS150 (a two-day bike ride totaling 150 miles to support Multiple Sclerosis) turned into a wardrobe of Spandex and training for several long-distance rides. Over the next three years, I spent days in spin classes and on the road, piling on 100–200 miles a week at the peak of training. I effortlessly found energy for training, pushing myself as hard as possible in preparation for the demanding Colorado terrain. I rode multiple charity and organized rides that were fifty-plus miles, and, in July 2009, I took on one of the most difficult amateur bike rides in Colorado called the Triple ByPass. It is a one-day 120-mile ride, climbing three mountain passes and totaling 10,000 feet of elevation gain. Crazy? Yes. And the miles were the easy part.

I started my journey at five a.m. and reached the first mountain pass just after sunrise. At 11,000 feet the air is cold—then descending at 30–40 mph is absolutely frigid. I had to carry enough clothes for the downhill but also be light enough for the rest of the day. The hardest part during the morning was maintaining caloric intake and hydration. I packed as much as I could, but it wasn't enough. As a first-timer, I was slower and inexperienced, and aid stations were too far apart for me. On the seven-mile uphill prior to lunch, I was out of Gatorade and my body craved real food and calories.

My body seemed to be eating itself. By the time I got to the lunch station, the food was pretty picked over. But I got a peanut butter sandwich and more energy bars.

After eating lunch and allowing my body some recovery time, I climbed the second of three mountain passes, Loveland Pass, to get over the Continental Divide. This day was no different than many other Colorado days—the weather on one side of the Divide was totally different than the other. Sunshine and warm temperatures turned to clouds, dropping temperatures, and rain, which then turned to hail. For four hours, I rode in the cold, pouring rain. My body was saturated. My sub-120 pound body was frozen to the core. I couldn't feel my feet, I couldn't feel my fingers, and I could barely see the road as rain pelted my face. My body shook to keep warm. During what was supposed to be a glorious celebration down Vail Pass, a bunch of us riders gathered under a bridge to do push-ups to warm our muscles. Unlike pedaling uphill, riding downhill lets your muscles cool down. I was so cold that I couldn't stop crying. I had spent ten hours climbing 102 miles of steep mountain grade, dreaming of the eighteen-mile downhill, and now all I wanted to do was go back up hill.

It was an anti-climactic arrival into Avon, Colorado to conclude the ride. Aaron had a bouquet of flowers waiting for me, which was super sweet, but I just cried. I was so exhausted. I had booked a hotel room for the night specifically because it had a hot tub. Thank goodness, because it relaxed my muscles and thawed my body! The next morning I went for a ninety-minute massage. As I filled out the therapist's form, it showed an outline of the human body asking to indicate which area needed attention. I circled the whole body. I hurt that badly.

We drove home to Denver and hung my bike up in the garage where it stayed for a long time. In the time between signing up for the Triple ByPass and riding it, my perspective had been shifting. By the time I hung up the bike, I was beginning to see the obsessive pattern.

I now know I rode the Triple ByPass because when I was on my bike I couldn't feel the pain of endometriosis. It took every ounce of energy to ride up the mountain, and I didn't care. Riding was all I could think about. It hid the pain from me—and ruined my body at the same time. My body already required extra energy to function with chronic pain, then I used any energy reserves to power up those mountains. My body was more tired than I ever knew. I now understand that it was not healthy. But back then, I would do anything to make the endometriosis pain go away, even if that meant enduring a different type of pain and exhaustion.

Hiding behind the mask of sports and physical exertion was a short-term fix. A way to survive. But it had become a long-term way of life—and it was hurting me. The slow transition to change was barely noticeable—until one day the ticking time bomb was out of time.

———

Just as cycling taught me that my mask hurt me physically, around the same time, losing my job taught me how the mask hurt me socially and professionally. After the late 2007 laparoscopy surgery, I headed into a rapid downward spiral of pain, increased medication, and decreasing quality of life. Not surprisingly, when the economy bottomed out of the architecture and construction industry in late 2008, I was one of the first to go.

I had gone from an aspiring designer on the most sought-after project in the region, to someone who was completely unreliable and calling in sick constantly. When I actually showed up to the office, pain pills left it hard to remember what was expected of me. But again, I thought I hid it well and believed that, when I was working, I was doing great. After all, I mastered the skill of putting on a pretty face and pretending. And to me, everything was fine. On days when I went to work, I would ride my bike. I needed to get in miles for the Triple ByPass, remember? Besides, the commute to work was less than two miles, which is nothing on a road bike. Not at all confusing for an employer: *This chick is in so much physical pain she can barely work, but she can easily ride a bike?*

Are you following my psyche? *If I can accomplish physical feats, then I am fine. If I am fine, I can continue to function in society* . . . until I can't. When this vicious cycle of proving to myself I was fine came crashing down, it crashed hard. Everything I knew about myself and about dealing with the disease crumbled. As much as I was hiding my illness from other people, I was hiding it from myself.

I spent years pretending to be normal. I did everything, consciously and unconsciously, to prove nothing was wrong with me. I didn't want to be sick. I never wanted any of this crap. I resented the idea of being the broken girl. The disconnection between my head and my heart grew so large that I completely lost myself. I was ashamed, and I covered it all up. But my body had something to say and was determined to be heard.

Now, years later, I can see how this pattern would not only be confusing for others, but also that it had to come to an end. For years I ignored the signs. Hell, I didn't even know signs existed. I didn't know I was scared or angry. I didn't know I was frightened to discover what was really going on. I was living a lie.

The realization and choice to change didn't happen overnight. Obviously my cycling obsession fizzled out after the Triple ByPass, and other tendencies slowly tapered off as my perspective started shifting. Recognizing my patterns and my mask was the first step.

What do you do to escape from pain? What helps you forget? Like me, you may allow others to see only certain parts of who you are and hide the rest from yourself and others. In an unconscious effort to survive and find normalcy, we ignore ourselves and invalidate our thoughts and feelings.

Wearing the mask by overachieving and overcommitting myself cost me energy, personal relationships, and most importantly, the connection to who I am. I resented the hormonal and emotional storms. All of the traumas made me hate my body and parts of myself. As the mask slowly came off, I began to understand how interconnected physical pain and emotional distress can be. Buried deep inside my psyche was more hurt than I ever knew.

I often wonder if I would have arrived at a pain-free life earlier if I would have just stopped overexerting myself. What if I had taken the mask off sooner?

chapter 4

the cereal bowl that changed everything

The fear of suffering is worse than suffering itself.
—Paulo Coehlo

woke up one awful morning in January 2009 at lord knows what time. I may have showered; I may not have. I do remember being in my usual University of Denver sweatshirt and yoga pants, my go-to I-feel-like-hell uniform. I rolled out of bed and sauntered into the kitchen, most likely to make tea. I wasn't eating much during the day; tea was about the only thing I felt like ingesting.

As I turned the corner to the kitchen, I found a cereal bowl sitting on the counter just above the dishwasher. My body tightened with irritation, and I instantly got a headache. My husband. *Ugh! Seriously? How hard is it to put a bowl IN the dishwasher? It's right there! Open the door, and put the bowl inside. Just open, and put the bowl inside the dishwasher. Are you *#$@% kidding me! You can't just open it and put the bowl INTO the dishwasher? You got up from the table, brought the bowl over to the sink, rinsed it out, and then sat it on the counter. But putting the bowl INTO the dishwasher was FAR too much to ask? Doing YOUR dishes is EXACTLY what I wanted to do today.*

I swear my head spun off my shoulders and orbited into outer space. At this point, I was beyond hysterical about a lonely bowl occupying space on the counter. I found my phone and dialed Aaron. He answered.

Not only was I yelling, but I was also *screaming* at him, "SERIOUSLY? You couldn't just open the dishwasher and put your cereal bowl inside?" I cried.

"Huh?" he replied.

"Put the BOWL in the DISHWASHER—too hard?!"

"Aud, I was running late. Just leave it. I'll do it when I get home."

"NO!" I snapped. "I don't want shit laying all over the house. Why couldn't you just put it in the dishwasher?" My emotions boiled over, and I was ugly-crying as I heard him take a deep breath and exhale.

"I don't know, Love. I am sorry. I am at work; I really cannot talk right now."

"WHATEVER!"

"Why don't you take something and lay down for a nap? We'll talk about it when I get home."

"GAH!" I cut him off and hung up.

I bawled myself into our bedroom where next to my side of the bed lived a basket full of orange pill bottles. I knew the contents all too well. Even half asleep, I could dig through the myriad bottles to find which pain pill, muscle relaxer, hormone, mood stabilizer or whatever else I wanted, take it, roll over, and fall back to sleep. Completely automatic. I knew the size, shape, and texture of each pill. I knew which combination would cut pain the quickest or last the longest. I knew which pills would keep me awake or put me to sleep.

There I was, sitting on the edge of my bed, staring at the basket. I could barely see through the stream of tears. Fury, anger, and hatred boiled inside of me. I'd pick each bottle up, hold it for a while, and consider how it would make me feel. Tossing each of them on the floor, I felt more and more deflated. I went through the whole basket, never taking anything. Nothing in there was going to solve my problem.

I stared down at the floor in disbelief. A pile of empty medical promises stared back at me. A pile of take-this-it-will-help-you-feel-better pills lay in front of me, and all I felt was infinite emptiness. I no longer knew if *I* felt tired or if a medication made me tired, if *I* felt fat and bloated or if that was just another side effect. Nothing in those orange pill bottles was going to *really* take away pain or stop the chaos inside my head. How did things get this out of control?

It's hard to revisit that desperate place, to understand just how angry and explosive my brain had become. I thought my day was ruined because of a singular cereal bowl sitting on the kitchen counter. Plus, I thought verbally unloading on my husband while he was at work was going to help. Unbelievable! It's hard to comprehend that, at the time, I thought all the medicines were helping me, that I was healthier and in a better place because of them. In reality, the side effects had taken over. I had lost control of my own body and emotions.

Sitting on the side of my bed that day and crying uncontrollably, I admitted to myself that I had been trying to get well for over half my life. I was no better off at that moment than I was at age 14 when it all began. So I quit.

I had to stop the frantic chaos inside me. I needed a new direction, to veer into the unknown. I knew I was going to feel pain. But I was feeling pain even with all the medicines. What did I have to lose?

The pills were supposed to take away my pain—they were supposed to do a lot of things, but in reality they were only assisting in the increasing disconnection between my head and my heart. As I stared at the pile of pill bottles that day, I chose to truly feel my pain. I chose to feel everything I'd been running from. I chose to face my issues, slay my dragon, and overcome my "something." I chose to feel my pain over the tingling numbness, fogginess, and forgetfulness of prescription pain pills. No more loading up and passing out. No more max doses by noon. No more me and the chemicals. No more dragging around the baggage of pain and disease. From that day forward, I chose to just be myself.

That day was the last day I ever considered taking a pain pill or muscle relaxer.

That day I stood up for myself. I didn't ask another doctor's or anyone else's opinion about what I should or shouldn't do. I didn't wait until there was "a good time" to consider my decision. Quitting pain pills came from a conventionally irrational place. In no way was I in the right mind to make a life-altering choice. But I did. I finally listened to a part of myself that had long been ignored. I gave voice to my emotional body, my internal wisdom, and my intuition.

I don't want to sugarcoat this as some heroic, courageous day that I triumphantly chose to take my life by the horns and start anew. That day was the worst day of my life. I sat there sobbing with a snotty, swollen face and feeling an angry rush of emotion. I was depressed. I was pissed. I was confused and scared. And yet I was motivated in a way that didn't yet make sense. I felt a fire burning that I didn't quite understand.

I didn't know what the hell I was going to do next, but I knew I couldn't keep doing what I was doing and expect different results. None of the pain pills, muscle relaxers, or hormones were prescribed to save my life. I didn't have some life-threatening whole-body infection that needed medication to stay alive. My prescriptions were supposed to be increasing my quality of life, and let me tell you, my quality of life sucked. I had given all my hopes for recovery to little pills filled with chemicals I didn't want to understand. In that moment, I realized life sucked with the pills, and it was going to suck without them. And I quit.

———

That same year, 2009, I was involved with a leadership program that met once a week. Participants were a variety of ages and from different backgrounds. Although I joined the program to grow as an entrepreneur and leader, much of what came up for me pertained to endometriosis and chronic pain. The underlying coursework was designed to work through our own head-trash to allow us space to move forward in our careers.

I had become friends with a man who ran the emergency department for one of the Denver hospitals. He knew I was dealing with endometriosis and would often ask how I was doing. A few weeks after quitting meds, he came up to me and asked how I felt. I commented that I had been feeling well. He just smiled and said, "I know. You look good."

"Thanks," I said with a confused look.

He continued, "How is life without pain pills?"

"Excuse me?" I answered, feeling a bit defensive, "How do you know what I am or am not taking?"

"Audrey, I'm an ER doc, it is my job to know within seconds what you are and are not taking. I can see it in your eyes. I'm proud of you."

To this day, that story makes me cry. He could see that the medicated fog had been lifted. He could see clarity returning. He could see power and self-confidence returning. He could see me becoming connected and grounded within my own body. The ironic thing is, I can now see it, too. I talk to so many women with endometriosis and chronic pain, and I can see it, too. I can see the fogginess and disconnection. It's not because I'm formally trained to know how medications affect the body; it's because I know the fog so well.

chapter 5

layers of pain

An emotion does not cause pain. Resistance or suppression of emotion causes pain.
—Fredrick Dodson, Parallel Universe of Self

Once the fog lifts, everything becomes clearer. Time has a way of bringing order to chaos. When I was living the chaos and pain of endometriosis, nothing made sense. I was grasping at anything and everything for help. Now, it all makes sense. I've learned endometriosis caused many layers of pain. Just like an onion, layer after layer of symptomatic issues, physical pain, lifestyle limitations, limiting beliefs, and trauma tightly wound into a ball of barbed wire, sharply cutting at every move.

For me, healing the disease was all about discovering layers of pain. Initially, endometriosis tissue is the base layer, causing the first wave of pain, dysfunction, and destruction. As abnormal cells grow outside the uterus and adhere to other organs, pain and/or dysfunction are the first warning signs. As endometriosis pain and destruction wears on, muscles around the uterus tighten to protect the organ. Over time, this constant state of protection and tension hardens muscles, creating a layer of scar tissue. That scar tissue hinders blood flow, effectiveness, and flexibility of muscles. Inflexible muscles affect connective tissue as well. Connective tissue supports organs by holding them in place. When this tissue becomes entangled and rigid, it creates another layer of pain.

Think about an old, neglected home. The wood floors and door frames start to lose moisture, drying out, and looking tired and cracked. Soon dust collects and spider webs form in the corners. In the home's glory days, it only took a quick mopping and dusting to restore its beauty. But after years of neglect, it takes deep cleaning, scrubbing, sanding, oiling, and restoration to bring back the shine.

Just like the old, neglected house, hardened, immobile muscles cannot be fixed with pain pills, muscle relaxers, or hormones. Chemicals cannot penetrate years of dust, spider webs, and neglect called scar tissue. Scar tissue and hardened connective tissue require special attention. Bodywork therapies such as connective tissue physical therapy, medical massage, and trigger point release therapy help to break up hardened tissue and restore healthy, relaxed tissue.

Long-term muscle immobility creates poor posture habits. If you think again of the old, neglected home, after long years of neglect, the roof starts to sag, the floor begins to cave, maybe the front porch sinks into the ground. The home can no longer support itself. The body is the same way.

Unhealthy posture has its own layer of pain and discomfort. I spent a lot of time curled up in the fetal position to find comfort. My muscles weakened and formed accordingly, resulting in rounded shoulders, slouchy posture, and feeble lower back muscles. Between chiropractic care and physical therapy rehabilitation, I've been rebalancing and rebuilding my muscular system to properly support my body. With all these layers of physical pain, limitations built. Negative thoughts built. Stress built. Traumatic experiences built. Layer after layer.

Western Medicine did not address the many layers causing pain for me. Beyond the elimination of endometriosis tissue, I felt lost and alone. Bit by bit, I realized it was up to me. Bit by bit, I began to understand my own layers of physical and emotional issues. After the breakdown of Cereal Bowl Day, I ever so slowly began to learn what my onion looked like. I began to discover myself, love myself, and do what is best for myself.

I've developed an illustration called the Pain Layers Diagram (download your copy of the diagram and worksheet at www. rewired-life.com/pain-layers-diagram). The Pain Layers Diagram illustrates the correlation between the pain in the physical body *and* emotional body for sufferers of endometriosis. The diagram is designed to start the conversation about what else could be contributing to the struggle of living with pain and disease. Every woman is different. The goal of the diagram is to see the disease as a whole, to see our body as a whole, and to begin to understand how each layer is related. For me, understanding that layers exist helped me see that every aspect of life affects health. I began to see every choice as an opportunity to do what is best for me and my health.

The emotional body and subsequent layers is where the most learning and healing took place for me. The first step in listening to my body was recognizing and learning where to look for emotional stress. I've identified four categories to begin exploring: emotional stress, emotional trauma, outside stresses, and negative thoughts and beliefs.

I define emotional stress as reactions to challenges or tension. Examples include: feeling like no one understands, anxiety around when your period is coming and what could potentially be ruined because of it, or sadness about missing out. I remember the anxiety I felt as my period grew near. There was no avoiding it; the little packet of birth control pills reminded me every month. I stressed about what was on my schedule. What could I get done beforehand, what was unavoidable, and what was going to inevitably be ruined. Yet again, my period ruled my life, reinforcing anxiety for next month. Without fail, compounding stress, anxiety, and disappointment layered onto my discomfort.

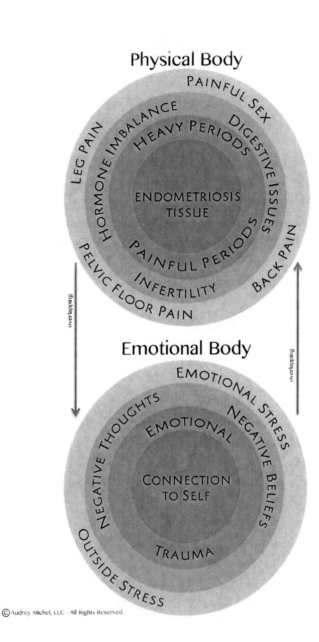

Physical Body

PAINFUL SEX
LEG PAIN
HORMONE IMBALANCE
HEAVY PERIODS
DIGESTIVE ISSUES
ENDOMETRIOSIS TISSUE
PAINFUL PERIODS
BACK PAIN
INFERTILITY
PELVIC FLOOR PAIN

overlapping

Emotional Body

EMOTIONAL STRESS
NEGATIVE THOUGHTS
EMOTIONAL
NEGATIVE BELIEFS
CONNECTION TO SELF
TRAUMA
OUTSIDE STRESS

The second emotional layer, outside stresses, are other people's opinions and projected expectations that affect our own stress and shame. Some of my outside stresses were the result of questions or statements from other people, such as:

"Have you seen a specialist?"

"Are you sure you are doing everything you can?"

"Maybe you should have a hysterectomy."

"You don't look like you feel very good."

"When are you having kids?"

The tough part about outside stresses is the inherent unpredictability. It didn't matter how people approached the topic—questions and opinions about motherhood sent me into an emotional tailspin. Once, while I was home for the holidays, someone asked "the kiddo question" at a bar. Where could I hide in a social situation like that? I hid behind sarcasm and revenge: "Oh, you didn't know? I was diagnosed with a painful reproductive disease at age 14. We don't know if we will be able to have kids."

Many times, the most hurtful outside stresses activate internal shame triggers. Shame is a powerful and damaging emotion. Everyone's shame triggers are different and unique to our experiences. The layers under shame are negative thoughts and beliefs. This encompasses deeply ingrained negative self-talk we no longer notice, as well as negative thoughts and beliefs we have picked up from the culture around us. A few examples of negative beliefs include thinking, *I'm not a good enough wife, mother, or friend*; experiencing guilt around exhaustion; or feeling self-consciousness around lack of intimacy. Many times resentment toward the body because of pain or health struggles, and even anger about missing out on life, are common among women with endometriosis.

For me, growing up in a working-class Midwestern town with a predominantly farming background, the role for females was very much defined by progress toward motherhood and the ability to keep a household running. So my dislike for my female parts, as well as rejection of the gender roles I'd been taught, caused major internal and relational conflict.

Lastly, I define emotional trauma as a severely distressing event or series of events such as a cyst bursting, severe hormone treatments, painful medical procedures, surgeries, or fertility issues. The night my cyst burst is a night I will never forget. Late in the evening of Thanksgiving 1995, I awoke to crippling pain. I remember crawling to the base of the stairs so my parents could hear my breathless yelps for help. Off to the emergency room we went. Doctors had told me, "When it ruptures, you'll know." And I did.

After drugs kicked in, I didn't remember much until we were back home, and the aftermath of a ruptured cyst began. Ongoing pain and exhaustion as well as dark, heavy blood oozed out of me for almost three months. I remember my mom commenting that she'd never purchased so many feminine products in her life. The extreme blood loss made me tired and anemic, which made me even more tired. It's no wonder that at fourteen I disliked my lady parts. None of the boys would ever have to experience this. The ruptured cyst, as well as numerous invasive medical procedures and drastic hormone treatments, left my body and mind traumatized in ways that took years for me to acknowledge.

In the coming chapters, we will dig deeper into these emotional layers. At this point, I want you to be aware that the ideas exist and have great potential to affect our mental and physical states, and manifest as pain or other issues.

———•———

Discovering and acknowledging emotional stresses and trauma, both from my past and in the current moment, has been confronting and difficult. I had some hefty issues to look at, and it was terrifying, and even overwhelming, to figure out what to do with the new information. As I started recognizing issues like the anxiety at the start of my period, remembering the trauma of a bursting cyst, or being blindsided by the kiddo question, my first step was to learn to be at ease. I do my best not to make the situation or myself bad or wrong. It is just information to know, not to judge. I take a deep breath to get centered so I can accept where I am in the current moment without judgment. I had to learn to love myself through these tough times.

In the beginning of practicing being at ease, it was hardest for me to accept a process I hated—my period was coming and my plans may not work out. The shift started with changing my verbiage. Did you catch what I said? I referred to my period as *a process I hated*. That's definitely not a judgment-free statement. We all have control over the words we speak. Shifting my perspective meant shifting my words. (Try catching yourself speaking or having negative thoughts—you'll be surprised how often you do it and don't even notice).

This shift was important. I could have chosen to revert to my old habits, bury the information, overreact, or find another "quick fix." But I've learned to sit with the information and discomfort without making it mean anything. There is not something for me to do; there is something for me to know and to learn. It's quite a test of patience to sit with anxiety or ugly feelings and be okay with it. It's about honoring where I am. It's about loving myself in the current moment. Loving myself unconditionally throughout the ups and downs, on ugly days as much as on wonderful days.

On the days when anger seemed to pour out of me, I did my best to greet it with ease and without judgment. Some days I wanted to tell the whole world to screw off, and that was okay. I embraced the feelings as a part of where I was for that day—and trusted I wouldn't be there forever. Hating hatefulness just infused more negativity, despair, and dislike for the situation. It's fairly common knowledge that depression leads to physical exhaustion and pain, and ongoing physical pain leads to exhaustion and depression. So shifting my thoughts became (and still is) so important.

When anger pours out of us, when we feel overwhelmed and stressed, our bodies cannot repair themselves. Only when our bodies are in a state of rest can healing occur. When I am in a shitstorm of emotions, my initial instincts aren't always love, acceptance, and ease. Many times, frustration or avoidance comes first. But I know the sooner I can love and accept myself in the current state of mind, the sooner I can truly move through the issue. The longer it takes me to find unconditional self-love, the longer I will be stuck in the vicious cycle of emotional stress and physical pain.

Discovering and acknowledging what lived in my psychological blind spot about endometriosis, chronic pain, and any other stressful or traumatic life events began to connect how emotions affected me physically. Throughout my life with endometriosis, I had experienced so many emotions, many of which I didn't understand. Yet the more I suppressed my emotional needs, the more pain manifested physically. And the more my body hurt, the more upset and depressed I felt. Getting out of that toxic rhythm was like getting off a spinning carousel.

Healing from endometriosis and chronic pain started when I began to pay attention to my emotional body. However, at the time, I thought I was simply looking for new tools for self-discovery and self-care, such as relaxation techniques for muscle spasms or sharp ovulation pain. But as I was learning how to work through emotional ups and downs of PMS and what foods were best for my body, I was learning how one layer affected another.

If we do not do the internal work to allow stress and trauma to move through us, those experiences can get stuck in our bodies. With time, the chances of stuck negative emotional energy manifesting as a physical issue increases. Thus, the cycle continues and we get trapped and suffocated by our own layers of stress and trauma. Layer after layer of small hurts, whether physical or emotional, can add up to seemingly insurmountable pain, illness, and disease.

When I started changing, I knew I was making new choices. I knew my choices were helping me gain my life back. I just didn't realize the small daily choices were assisting my whole body in healing.

Recognizing that physical pain causes emotional trauma, and that emotional trauma causes physical pain, takes courage. If we break the cycle, we change the trajectory of our pain and the outcome of wellness for the better.

chapter 6

reconnecting wires

*Sometimes you don't realize your own strength until you
come face to face with your greatest weakness.*
—Susan Gale

After the breakdown of Cereal Bowl Day, I made a lot changes. I decided feeling okay wasn't good enough. Calling pain level 5 a good day wasn't good enough. Average wasn't good enough. After choosing to quit pain meds, I felt more and more like myself. More clear. More calm. More grounded. It had been so long since I'd felt free of heavy fog and cloudiness. I wanted to feel more alive. I wanted to be more connected to myself, to my friends and family, and to my environment. Wasn't it time for something better? Didn't I deserve better? Didn't I owe myself better?

What began as a short-term fix—pain pills and hormones— became a lifelong pattern that built the Berlin Wall between my head and my heart. It was time for the wall to come down.

I had never been much of a reader, but after learning about the head-trash concept in my leadership training program, I wanted to know more. I made it my new to job to read any self-help book I could find, redefining what wellness meant to me. I read the books, I did the exercises, and I challenged my perspective. I decided to rewire my life.

I discovered a new world, a new way of thinking. I had to figure out how to reconnect myself with my body and emotions when all I'd ever done was shut down the possibility of knowing my body and myself. Western medicine can certainly stop a condition or illness from progressing. In fact, Western medicine is why I was diagnosed so early, which is rare. Would the endometriosis have spread if we didn't catch it when I was fourteen? We will never know for sure. However, for years none of the prescriptions ever fixed my problems, eliminated pelvic and back pain, or smoothed out my roller coaster of emotions. I placed all my hope in every treatment and every new prescription.

After quitting, I realized my hopes were misplaced. Hitting rock bottom and being forced to re-evaluate my life was the best thing to happen to me. I thrust myself into learning new ways of assessing my health and new ways of being. Everything was an a-ha moment. I turned my focus from "just make the pain go away" to curiosity, self-discovery, and whole body health.

On the epic day that my emotional body stood up for itself, I not only quit pain pills, but I also quit ignoring myself. I chose to acknowledge, "Yup, I'm in pain, and I am okay." This time, instead of spraying Febreze on the rotten pile of cow dung and closing the door to that part of my life, I decided to see why it stunk so badly in the first place. I chose to ask why my *whole being* hurt. Instead of being defeated, victimized, and always asking why, I was now curious about what was really going on with me. I began asking tough questions of myself that only I could answer. I finally took responsibility for myself and took action to take care of all of me.

The process of reconnecting is like discovering a diamond in the rough. The process of cutting and polishing a diamond is abrasive. Self-discovery is uncomfortable, and it is real. As much as I yearned for a bright shiny future, I still had to dig myself out of the mud and do the work. For me, reconnecting and self-discovery came from new insights, learning new tools, and implementing lasting change into my life.

One step toward reconnecting and whole-body wellness

came when friends gave me a gift card to see an acupuncturist for three visits. In year's prior, I had seen chiropractors that also did acupuncture, and although my energy seemed to have increased, I didn't necessarily see overall results. Needless to say, I was skeptical of the gift. In reviewing the practitioner's website, I discovered her practice included techniques I'd never encountered. I had never been to a practitioner with a Traditional Chinese Medicine background who used sensing techniques to select needle locations. It all sounded very abstract. So in the spirit of being open to new experiences, I said yes. If my friends felt strongly enough to pay for three visits, I should at least give it a try.

The general theory of acupuncture is based on the premise that an energy called Qi (pronounced *chee*) regulates bodily functions. Qi is believed to be the life force and vital energy of the universe. Traditional Chinese Medicine believes that Qi is fundamental to all aspects of life and that disease rises from disruptions and the imbalance of one's energy. An acupuncturist takes into consideration physical symptoms and emotional states along with environmental factors to understand energy disruptions. Stimulating specific acupuncture points corrects imbalances through meridians, or channels, in which Qi flows in the body.

Traditional Chinese Medicine believes emotions and traumatic experiences get stuck in the body; acupuncture assists in releasing the stuck, stagnant emotions and experiences. Emotions are the embodiment and perceptions of our life experiences, and emotions are considered energy. An acupuncturist places needles at certain points that correspond with meridians, or energy pathways, to rebalance and unblock the flow of Qi within the body.

Let me tell you, when I was researching acupuncture to decide if it was for me or not, I didn't know what the hell this all meant. Meridian this, Qi that . . . I didn't even know these things existed. And I definitely didn't know having them balanced was essential to my wellness.

My first acupuncture appointment began with an initial

evaluation. The acupuncturist, Christine, asked about pain levels, emotional status, and my diet, as well as my daily routine and struggles: Have you been sleeping? How is your diet and digestion? Where are you at with your menstrual cycle? Pretty normal stuff.

She then checked my pulse and the appearance of my tongue. In Traditional Chinese Medicine pulses are taken at three depths at three different locations to give insight into how the body is functioning. The tongue is also a diagnostic tool; observing color and general condition provides information about possible disharmony within the body. That was new to me. I lay on the table, much like a massage table, and she began the process of sensing meridians and energetic blockages. She touched my feet or shoulders and squeezed my legs or arms, looking and listening to my body. As she did this, she knew where to place the needles. I was surprised that being poked with acupuncture needles was totally different than medical needles. I barely noticed it was happening. (I actually called them pins, not needles—it sounds less harsh). When Christine was satisfied with the number of pins and their locations, she let me be, allowing time for the treatment to integrate and energy to move accordingly.

Many times acupuncture appointments include other therapies such as craniosacral therapy, visceral manipulation, moxibustion, and cupping, as well as herbs to take home to continue supporting whatever the treatment started. All of these components of acupuncture are used to treat the whole person– mind, body, and spirit.

Hadn't I been treating my whole body for years? Birth control and pain pills for my uterus and ovaries. Muscle relaxers for my back. Miralax for digestion. Mood stabilizers for my emotions. Sleeping pills for rest. Trust me, my whole body needed something! But alternative healing felt different. It felt *real* in every sense of the word. My digestion was working because my digestive system *was working*, not because some pill had turned poo into water for the sake of getting rid of it. No, I didn't want bodily waste backed up for days, but I didn't want pee-butt either. That was just as awful. But giving my digestive system the balance it needed to do its job, now that is wellness.

Christine was the first practitioner to ask questions such as;

"How do you feel after eating *xyz*?"

"When you feel tired, do you allow your body to rest?"

"How are you feeling emotionally this week?"

"When you get stressed, where do you feel it in your body?

Ummm . . . what? Everything about acupuncture was making me think. In the days following acupuncture appointments, I felt improvements. I could feel that it was working. My body craved the treatment, and I looked forward to my next appointment. Christine never treated me like *endometriosis*. She treated me like a real person, with real problems. That's the holistic and intuitive nature of acupuncture—treating every person as a one-of-a-kind case.

I remember one of the first serious conversations Christine and I had after she asked all of her initial questions.

"How's sleep, how's digestion, how are your emotions . . ."

"The same. I don't know. Better, maybe."

She took a deep breath, and I braced myself for the "You Aren't Taking This Seriously" talk. What she said next stuck with me.

"Audrey, you call a pain level of 5 a good day. You seem to think *fine* is good enough. It's not good enough, and any pain is too much pain. I've helped many people get out of just as painful situations. I know I can help you, too. But I need your help. You're going to have to feel where you hurt. You cannot use pain as a blanket descriptor any longer."

That pissed me off. I went home and wrote a journal entry spewing anger about how badly I did *not* want to know the nuances about how I felt. *"My whole body hurts all the time. What different does it make where or when I feel what?"* As I rambled about how stupid all this was, I wrote something that stopped me in my tracks: "It [describing pain] never helped in the past, why would it help now?" Exactly! Why would it help now?

For years, I used "pain" as a blanket descriptor. During the years of intense physical pain, the most annoying and irritating thing anyone could ask me was, "How is your pain today compared to yesterday?" I didn't want to think about the answer, consider the nuances of how I felt, or describe it. I usually responded like a super annoyed teenager who'd rather be doing anything other than talking to you: "My pain level is a 10. It hurts everywhere, and I hurt every day. Thanks for reminding me!" *Ugh!*

To prove my point to Christine, I took out my day planner and started taking notes on what I ate, how much I slept, how long my period lasted, pain levels and location, and described it all. I was even more pissed, but I told myself I'd do this until my next appointment, at that point proving how stupid it was and quit.

It didn't go that way. Owning the disease began with describing it.

Christine found it really helpful, and so did I. I learned that a period shouldn't be super heavy for three days, continue for another two, and linger for a couple more, finally quitting after seven. I didn't know that. That's the way it had always been, so when asked about my period, I would say, "Fine." I learned not pooing for three or four days wasn't fine either. My long history of subpar health left me complacent. I could go nine days without pooing, so three days was like heaven. I also discovered there was difference in the pain I experienced.

"My eyelashes hurt," explained the overall painful, tired, and taking-all-my-energy-to-exist feeling. Those days were an all-over fatigue, the kind of exhaustion where asking me to move from the bed to the sofa was far too much. If my phone wasn't within reach, I probably wouldn't answer it. If food wasn't put in front of my face, I probably wouldn't eat. Basically, I was too tired, and it was the type of pain that took too much energy to lift even my eyelashes. "My eyelashes hurt" type of pain was usually associated with menstruation.

Also I noticed that with "My eyelashes hurt" pain, the PMS

emotional roller coaster started days before any sign of my period and lasted days after my cycle had ended. I had fear and anxiety about the timing of my period and how it was going to affect life, which added another layer of issues. I also noticed I had a horrible diet around menstruation. I craved junk food like you wouldn't believe. When I did have the energy to get up, you did not want to get between Burger King and me. All I wanted was a double cheeseburger meal, plain, with a Diet Coke. Watch out!

The "Meat Grinder" described when ovulation felt like my organs were being shoved through a meat grinder. I could *feel* which ovary was supplying barbed wire wrapped eggs to my uterus; it felt like my body was pushing a boulder up a mountain. Pain sharply stabbed my abdomen and lower back and then radiated out to the rest of my limbs. My uterus and ovaries were being chopped up and spit out by the "Meat Grinder". It was dizzying and debilitating.

The PMS roller coaster doesn't even begin to describe how crazy and irritable I could be. "Psycho bitch" was the term I lovingly used to describe the emotions that would explode out of me. When I think about it, I often wonder how I am still married. My husband is a patient man!

Now I could describe my condition in a couple of specific words. *Meat Grinder.* Between Christine, my chiropractor, and massage therapist, everybody knew exactly how I felt, and, more importantly, I didn't have to answer the laundry list of questions. Describing pain was the beginning of reconnecting me to my body, and I got to know it on a new level. I was curious about why I felt the way I did beyond physiology.

Instead of tackling the beast of endometriosis and chronic pain, we started with easier feats, such as realigning my sleeping schedule and eliminating junk food. The method of treating small problems of everyday life (e.g., sleep, diet, digestion, anxiety) helped me see gradual improvements. Small victories helped me maintain a positive outlook and hope for a better future. As my body improved, so did my emotions, and as my emotions improved, so did my body. Stress and tension melted away, and I felt more energy. As time went on, my hormones and emotions smoothed out. The number of days I was stuck in bed decreased. I was less cranky and began to participate in life. I *felt* like being active again.

Christine's ability to hear me and intuitively feel my body's needs kept me coming back. I felt like Christine was teaching me a new language, and I loved it. When I was ready to dip my toe into the pond of hearing the voice of my emotional body, I knew she was safe and supportive. The next step was to do what was right for me and to trust that my intuition and inner wisdom knew what was best.

Acupuncture overlapped with my "new job" of addressing stress and anxiety. Christine fit in perfectly. I began by speaking about my frustrations and my intuition. I no longer just answered Christine's questions I fearlessly expressed myself. To find my voice, I had to have an open dialogue, and Christine helped me begin to decipher the code. She never rushed me or cut me off. She just listened with empathy.

Christine was the first practitioner who fully listened, heard my struggle, and understood me on all levels. This trust was important. She helped me shift value back to me. Before, I had given the highest value to doctors' opinions. And when I would describe pain, I always wanted them to tell me why it hurt. When doctors stopped having answers, I stopped placing value on describing pain. Now, my voice was making a difference. Now, describing pain came from a place of authority and power. "This is how it feels for me" is a statement, not a question; a goal, not a problem to be fixed. With Christine, I had a partner. And I finally realized that if my gut tells me a practitioner doesn't get me, get out. There are plenty of people in the world ready and willing to help in a way that makes sense and works for you. How empowering!

chapter 7

inching into alternatives

We have a lot of inner unlearning and relearning to do.
—Tara Mohr, Playing Big

After several months of treatment, Christine asked if I was open to trying something different. I trusted her. Being in a place of complete desperation, combined with curiosity and a desire to learn, I was ready to try just about anything. I had no idea what she was up to, but everything she'd ever suggested had been helpful, so I agreed to participate. Unbeknownst to me, my body had something bubbling under the surface.

Putting one hand on my lower back and one on my stomach, she asked that we put our collective energy and attention on the space between her hands. She instructed me to simply notice what came up for me. Now, I was raised in a small town in the middle of Nebraska. Where I am from, we did not "go within," meditate, "listen" to our bodies, or anything else like that, so this was way outside my comfort zone, making me nervous and disoriented.

Christine was quiet for a while and then started asking questions. "Are you experiencing any thoughts or feelings? Are you seeing any images or colors? Are you having any sensations?" I just lay there in silence. I did my best to consider what she was asking, but literally, there was nothing. Nothing. Just emptiness.

Overwhelmed with emptiness and nothingness, I quietly

started to cry. Tears slowly filled up the corners of my eyes, dripped down my cheeks, and pooled in my ears. I felt an incredible silence. I could feel my heartbeat echoing throughout my cavernous, empty body. My consciousness was completely paralyzed. I couldn't even speak.

I don't know how long Christine let me lie there with my own thoughts before she finally asked again what I was experiencing.

"Nothing," is all I whispered through the tears. "Just nothing."

Christine knows when to push and when to accept where I am. She didn't say a word, but left me with my own thoughts.

When our session finished, she told me she wanted me to see someone, "A kinesiologist. Her techniques will allow you to continue to reconnect with your body and emotions on a deeper level."

I spent most of the rest of that day crying and spiraling with thoughts: *What did all this mean? What was I supposed to see or feel during the session? Why didn't I see anything? What's the matter with me?*

From what I've found, not many people grow up learning to truly move past stressful or traumatic events. I had been brought up with essentially two ways to deal with emotional distress. First, get over the issue and get on with life. Apparently, being strong means ignoring emotions, especially "bad" ones. Lord knows you don't want to be weak and show "crazy" emotions. And forget seeking out a therapist, because that definitely means you're crazy, and you don't want to be the one with issues. Second, let the experience define you. We all know someone who identifies as being the divorcee or the drug addict. If we never work through a traumatic experience, fight against it and make it the enemy, it can define us. The traumatic experience is the only lens we see through, and it determines how life occurs, hindering our ability to see the bigger picture.

When it came to pain and endometriosis, I chose the first option: I sucked it up and got on with life. I figured out how to tuck away pain, guilt, anger, and trauma. I didn't have time for those feelings. I was too busy overachieving to tend to emotional crap. I pretended stress and emotional pain never existed. If I were an amphibian, I would have just chopped off the unwanted parts of myself and grown new, untarnished emotional limbs. But humans aren't designed that way. Our cells and tissues hold stress and trauma, and unless we have tools to let go and heal, the trauma gets stuck. And trust me, disregarding or pretending trauma isn't there is not healthy, and it is definitely not healing.

In the spirit of learning new things and learning about myself, I said yes to seeing this kinesiologist whom Christine was suggesting. Again, just like acupuncture, I researched kinesiology and found out educational kinesiology specializing in emotional issues is a holistic discipline that also analyzes meridian energy lines. This type of kinesiology uses muscle-testing techniques to access the subconscious mind and gain information about certain issues within the body, mind, and spirit, in order to restore balance. Again, unsure of what it all meant, I trusted Christine, like I trusted my friends, and took a leap of faith.

Armed with complete innocence and ignorance, I showed up at a lovely lady's house and nervously sat at her kitchen table. I explained how I broke down at my last acupuncture appointment and needed help reconnecting with my body. This first appointment with Deb consisted of a lot of learning. I learned how muscle-checking discovers which areas of my body are holding emotional issues and negativity. With an emphasis on emotional issues, educational kinesiology focuses on fourteen meridians relating to our organs, all of which hold different emotions, meaning, and interpretations. Through these meridians, the emotional body communicates information. For example, the heart meridian communicates unconditional love, acceptance, and appreciation for yourself and others. The spleen represents an ability to relax, trust, and let go of anxiety, worry, and unforgiveness. Kidney meridians reveal safety issues such as whether or not it is safe for me to explore who I am or to remember past experiences. Over the years, kidney balances have been the most recurring for me. Muscle-checking helps uncover negative beliefs and thoughts from the past, present, or that we've projected into the future.

What I remember most is walking away from our first session feeling intellectually unsure of what just happened but feeling heaviness removed from my body. Weight was lifted. I stood taller. I felt clearer.

Our first order of business was for me to learn to "live in my own body." I had to be present, not living in the past or fearful of the future, but in this moment. This brought all my subconscious avoidance mechanisms to the forefront. I couldn't hide. I couldn't disconnect. The time had come to deal with all the layers of trauma from endometriosis and living with chronic pain. Surviving physical pain had been a fight-or-flight instinct, a need. Emotional healing, on the other hand, was a choice to look inward at why I react one way or another in different situations. It involved questioning what brings on stress or throws me into a breakdown. Emotional healing required unlearning many of the patterns I'd developed so I could adapt healthy ways of being. Never once had I considered why I was stuck in the first place; yet once I did, it reconnected every part of my being and began deep healing.

Working with Deb as my kinesiologist and spiritual leader, I learned a third option for dealing with life's challenges: listening to your body and giving voice to internal wisdom. One of the biggest realizations was that my emotional body (inner wisdom, body-mind, or whatever else you'd like to call it) is smarter than my brain. I could easily give my opinion or judgment about a situation, but that is an intellectual, head-oriented thought. Opinions and judgments have nothing to do with my heart or internal voice.

Every cell in my body holds emotion, experiences, and memories. Every cell in my body has the ability to tell me where I am stuck, where to go next, and what is best for me. Our bodies have much to tell us. It is a message board to our psyche, and when we can calm our minds, within the silence, we will hear what our bodies have to tell us. Our bodies will reveal all the right answers at all the right times. I had to slow down, stop, and look at my own insecurities and beliefs, and then lean into them. It was scary to break old patterns and peel back layers of hurt. Tackling emotional healing took a lot of courage. I had to dig in and question my own insecurities and fears. Yet the journey of reconnection became like a treasure hunt of self-discovery. And each new discovery made me feel lighter, freer, and more like myself.

I used to skim over stressful or hurtful events thinking, *I'm strong; it doesn't bother me.* I'd intellectually "forget about it." Now I know better. The ability to hear that my body is stressed or experienced trauma is invaluable. Understanding when I need a break or need to infuse self-care helps me be my best self. I've learned to be at ease and without judgment for my situation or myself. I show myself the same love and patience I would give a small child after experiencing something hurtful. Learning to acknowledge stress, and to then love myself through the ups and downs, was new for me—and hard.

I had felt isolated with endometriosis for so long. I didn't know anyone else with it. I intellectually knew millions of women suffered, but I didn't personally know anyone in my situation. As hard as my family and friends tried to be understanding and supportive, I didn't have anyone who "got" that part of me. I didn't have anyone in whom I could confide, ask questions, or guide me through the process of healing. Now I did! I had safe places and safe, empathetic people. And as I greeted the undesirable parts of myself with unconditional love, I had a team of people right next to me guiding me to real healing.

chapter 8

looking at gremlins

Fairy tales are more than true—not because they tell us dragons exist, but because they tell us dragons can be beaten.
—Neil Gaiman, Coraline

Recently, I smashed my thumb in the door as it closed. It wasn't broken; I just scraped off a large amount of skin. Man, did that hurt! For the first couple of days, it was difficult to bend, and it ended up taking over three weeks to heal. Never once did I look at my thumb with disgust or anger. Not once while it was awkward to maneuver did I force myself to overuse it. I simply altered my way of doing things for a bit while I trusted my body to heal my thumb and skin.

Why then, when it comes to emotional healing, did I struggle to allow myself time to heal? I still struggle with relaxing and trusting the timing my body needs because the idea that I should feel good and be happy every day was ingrained into my psyche. And if I don't, something is wrong with me that I had better fix now.

In so much of my life, I would avoid saying the word "endometriosis." Let's be honest, it's a hefty word loaded with a lot of history and emotion. It was quite likely I would be tearing up by the time I finished the sentence, "I have endometriosis." Prior to alternative healing, I never questioned such emotion. I just avoided it so it wouldn't come up. But after learning about listening to my body, I knew the emotion behind the word meant there was an opportunity for self-discovery, growth, and healing.

Kinesiology taught me to exhale, to allow my body the time it needed to process. As I considered my thought patterns and emotional issues, I began to wonder, *What if I listened to the tiny voice in my heart?* Not the voice telling me I'm not good enough or no one cares what I think—that is my inner critic, ego, or gremlins talking. That critical voice tended to be the loudest, but it's not the one I should be listening to. The voice of my heart hadn't been anything more than a whisper, yet it carried so much wisdom. This tiny voice tugged at me every time I took a pill. It told me that Prozac actually made me crazier. It gave an involuntary eye roll of irritation as doctors suggested another internal ultrasound to double-check that cysts weren't forming.

What if there was something to that inner wisdom? What if I sat quietly and asked my body, "What is it I need to know today?" What did I have to lose? Another round of Vicodin and yet another pelvic exam in the name of "my health"? I didn't need any of it, and finally I listened.

Just as I trusted my body to heal my smashed thumb, I had to trust that my emotional body would take care of emotional hurt as well.

———•———

For years I was trying so hard to figure out how to be healthy that I basically strangled the life out of any hope or possibility. It's no secret that ongoing stress leads to many health issues. I was like a crazy, frantic dog chasing its tail at 100 miles an hour. Calmness was not a sensation I was used to. Frantic, unhappy, overwhelming feelings allowed stress to take over. And I clung to any empty promise to fix me. But now it was time to find calmness within.

I got a taste for this calmness after my first kinesiology meeting with Deb. But unlearning unhelpful patterns had just begun, so it didn't take long for ugly feelings and heaviness to return. I was definitely used to running from the gremlins in my head.

How do you please a slimy green monster whose only job is to infuse self-doubt and criticism into your life? If you think you beat the gremlins, they just move onto the next opportunity for self-sabotage. Trying to please these guys is a waste of time. Yet running away isn't any better. So what do you do when option A and B don't work?

You find option C.

I couldn't please them; I couldn't run away from them, so what if I stopped and looked these gremlins in the eyes? What if I asked them what the hell they wanted? What if I listened to what they had to say? But to hear what they were saying, I had to be present within my own body. A body I hated. A body I resented. I had to learn that it was safe to be in my body and safe to look at my own issues. The gremlins weren't going to eat me . . . right?

Gremlins thrive in stressful, traumatic conditions. These gremlins represent negative thoughts and beliefs such as self-doubt, self-criticism, anger, resentment, negativity, shame, and guilt. I always think of Mucinex commercials with the green blob mucus characters that set up camp inside someone's lungs. You don't want them living in your sinuses, and you definitely don't want their cousins pitching a tent in your subconscious. The gremlin colony in my subconscious seemed to be partying every night—and breeding like rabbits. They had a cushy life for many years. But it was time to kick out these squatters. It was time for me to regain the lost real estate.

As I mentioned, I was scared to know the nuances of physical pain. A major gremlin for me to get to know was not only physical pain, but emotional pain, too. Once I broke the seal of talking about physical pain and admitting I wasn't fine, it became quite easy. Emotional pain, however, was much more difficult. These gremlins are really good at hiding and pretending they aren't there. Emotional pain is the queen of the gremlin community. I am grateful Deb knew it was best to break the task up into smaller, more manageable pieces. Confronting smaller gremlin families one at a time was less overwhelming.

The first gremlin family to look at was resentment of pain and disease. Even though I spent so many years pretending I was fine, in reality I was pissed about many things. I resented everything I missed out on because of pain. I resented how many memories were missing because medications made it hard to remember. I resented that many relationships suffered because of severe PMS and unstable behavior. I resented that many of my achievements and most of my life path had come from a place of fear. I resented my fear-based choices. I resented the amount of time I spent with my head buried in the sand. I often felt scared and overwhelmed by the ugly feelings bottled up inside of me. Realizing that hate, anger, guilt, resentment, and shame were stuck inside my body created a lot of sadness. Not until I considered the enormity of fifteen years of painful bottled up emotions did I actually start to comprehend the amount of resentment, anger, and hate I carried. Then I could feel and see the weight and destructiveness of ignoring these emotions.

For decades I believed that simply because I am female, I had to endure terrible pain. When the Universe handed out lady parts, I got the broken ones. I resented being a woman. To me, being a woman was reduced to having a uterus, ovaries, and a period, and none of mine functioned properly. All I'd ever known about womanhood was painful monthly cycles and a uterus lining that grew everywhere it wasn't supposed to. My body didn't function like other girls' bodies. A belief that my body only brought pain and dysfunction reinforced more pain and dysfunction. I hated my body, what endometriosis put me through, my period, and my reproductive organs. All that hate then made me angry. And I secretly feared that maybe there was more to come.

There was more to come, just not in the way that I had anticipated. The next family of gremlins to face was fear. I was (and still am to this day) scared of a lot of things. As Deb and I ousted this gremlin family, the first fear that presented itself was around life without medication. Pills were comfortable, and I had been scared to let go of the crutch. I soon learned my need for short-term comfort hindered my ability to experience overall success toward long-term health.

After quitting pain pills, I realized pain wasn't exponentially worse without medication, just different. With my shift in perspective, my priorities no longer aligned with letting fear of the future and fear of unimaginable pain be in control. A pain level of 10 without the medicated fog somehow felt like a slightly better version of 10. I felt physical pain just as I always had, but the fog was gone. I felt clear. It had been so long since I had felt even a little bit like myself, that this feeling far outweighed the idea of continuing to use pain medication.

As the medicated fog lifted, my connection to my body became stronger and my fears became weaker. A stronger connection to my inner self helped me more quickly see the fear-gremlins standing in my way. I was scared to consider what others would think about me lying to myself for so many years. I was scared to fully remove the mask and show my real feelings and emotions. Even though I was scared, I was okay. The lessons of being at ease and not making myself wrong for having fear-based feelings were sinking in. Instead of being scared of these feelings, I just acknowledged them. I was changing, and the shift felt good.

As the gremlin colony dissipated, love for my body and myself grew. Embracing my story of a bumpy journey to womanhood and dependence on medication took time. I slowly exposed the extent of resentment, fear, and other ugly emotions. There were, and continues to be, gremlins to confront. I'll cover this more in depth later, but for now, I wanted to acknowledge the enormity of recognizing hate and anger around being a woman. Understanding why I would love, accept, or embrace something that doesn't even work was revolutionary for me. Slowly, the feeling of being overwhelmed lessened. Step by step, looking gremlins in the eye became less scary. It was the end of compartmentalizing and burying endometriosis and chronic pain issues, and the beginning of embracing me. I find it amazing that I could comprehend unconditional love for another in need but struggled with unconditional love for myself. My kinesiologist and I went to work on loving and accepting my body in the current moment, even if in the current moment, it was in a state of disrepair.

———

From the outside, the process of confronting gremlins looked like a lot of tears, a lot of sleeping, and a lot of long showers. And to be honest, it probably looked like a mid-life crisis. I allowed emotions to come out of me, and it was exhausting. Part of kinesiology and spiritual work is to trust that whatever is showing up is exactly what is supposed to be showing up. Each month Deb and I met, we didn't necessarily have a perfectly laid out plan, but we had an overall direction and goal. Each session, my body presented the emotional issues it was ready to deal with, sometimes starting with simply following silly thoughts that popped into my head. In order to let go of head-oriented thoughts, I had to trust the unplanned words that flowed from my heart through my mouth. (Haven't you had moments where you didn't know the thoughts you thought until they spilled out of your mouth? I've learned to trust these moments as inner wisdom). Even at appointments when I thought I was doing well, we still found gremlins.

During one of the earliest appointments, I showed up to Deb's house feeling guilty for not standing up for myself or listening to my body sooner. Deb listened to my story and sat with me through the tears. She then began muscle-checking my meridians. As she pushed on my arm, my emotional body communicated where we needed to work. On this particular day, the first layer was a kidney issue. Deb was quiet for a minute and then asked, "What are you scared of?"

As tears bubbled up and a fire burned in my belly, the only thought inside of me was: *I am scared to know what it looks like to stand up for my true self. To be authentically and unapologetically me. My people-pleasing self is scared. I don't want to upset anyone or have someone think less of me.*

After talking through what this meant for me, she muscle-checked again to see if there was another issue. Sure enough, there was a large intestine issue.

"What do you need to let go of?" she asked.

This time, I sat for a minute, quietly listening to what my emotional body had to say. What came up? I felt I wasted many years of my life wearing the "I'm fine" mask. I felt stuck between trying to make sense of past experiences (I didn't want it all to be a waste) and simply letting it all go and starting anew. As soon as I said these words out loud, I knew what I needed to do. It was time to honor my past, time to thank it for its contribution and time to let it go.

That day we finished by working through several kinesiology techniques to integrate new knowledge and affirmations so the connections to these lessons were easily accessible in the future. Deb helped me let go of feeling embarrassed and ashamed. It helped me release the past, as well as guilt, for not recognizing and stopping destructive behaviors sooner. I embraced this self-discovery, excited to head in an unknown direction.

⸻

Although I was determined to be well, I was fearful and overwhelmed by the path in front of me. I knew gremlins lived in the dark shadows and rugged terrain. Deb helped me identify which gremlins I was ready to approach and then integrate small shifts and lifestyle changes. Little by little, endometriosis and chronic pain were no longer at the forefront of my life. Chaos and feeling overwhelmed dissipated, and stressful situations no longer had the upper hand.

Kinesiology quickly became an integral part of my healing. I initially thought kinesiology was an isolated therapy allowing me to deepen the connection to my emotional body and inner wisdom. But kinesiology was tandem and supportive to everything else. Kinesiology helped me to effectively communicate my needs to all my therapists. My muscles relax after releasing fear; allowing chiropractic and massage to restore muscle balance and acupuncture to move Qi. Kinesiology also helped me deal with emotional issues that popped up while on the acupuncture, chiropractic, or massage table. Kinesiology helped me feel safe as I progressed to becoming a healthy person.

———•

The concept of changing habits and overall perspectives sounds easy. You just choose to do things differently, like a New Year's resolution, right? Not really. Integrating real, lasting change is challenging. If creating lasting change for your life is important, begin by addressing low-hanging fruit– the easy stuff. Experiencing small wins creates progress and a feeling of forward movement. And that is essential to finding joy and healing.

Look around right now, what do you see that irritates you? That pile of shoes by the front door? Do you constantly tell yourself, your husband, your kids to move them? How easy would it be to get a shoe rack for the coat closet? Do you need to create a standard that in your house everyone puts his or her own shoes away? I know this sounds silly, being that I've been addressing heavy emotional crud and gremlins, endometriosis and chronic pain, but healing pain and disease is about healing life. If you are going to skim over your own feelings about something as insignificant as shoes lying around, how are you going to treat yourself when it comes to tough emotions? Start a practice of listening to your body and changing your environment, even on the little things. Trust me, it builds confidence and feels fantastic.

I want you to know it is possible to overcome whatever mountain or ravine you are facing. I know that there are times when getting out of bed deserves a medal. I know the desperate, helpless feeling. I also know the other side of pain and disease where real health and wellness is possible. The current moment doesn't have to be your forever.

Take control of your life, stand up for yourself, and let your voice be heard. Reconnecting is a process of learning to quiet your mind, listen to your body, and take action on what your body has to say. Looking within is about identifying your physical and emotional signs of distress and having courage to take one step at a time toward letting go, changing habits, and authentically loving and accepting yourself.

I recently interviewed women with varying stages of endometriosis, at varying lengths of diagnosis, about their emotional struggles. Dealing with day-to-day life was the overwhelming answer. "How do you be your best at work, at home, with the family, and with friends when exhaustion and pain is at its worst?" "How do you continue to show up to life when your body is tired, when your mind is tired, and you're just plain tired of being tired?"

My journey to wellness has forced me to consider how every aspect of life affects my body. I switch my mindset from what I didn't get done today or what I wasn't able to do to asking myself, "Have I done everything I can to help my body heal today? Am I giving myself the best chance at being well?" Changing my verbiage from, "I didn't finish doing everything I needed today" to "I didn't finish everything I wanted, and that is okay" has been key.

I've let go of a lot of stressful things that I thought were needs because of my own or others' expectations. I now question what is a "priority"? Answering all emails within 24 hours, nope. A perfectly spotless, clutter-free home, nope. A beautifully made-up, designer-magazine-like bed, nope. Always leaving the house showered, hair done, makeup done, coordinating outfit and shoes, nope. Showing up to every social and professional event I've previously committed to, nope. I learned to prioritize what is really a priority moment to moment. Then I let the rest go.

I started saying yes when my body tells me it needs a few minutes of rest. Choosing to accompany my lunch sandwich with pistachios instead of Doritos, yes. Joyously spending forty-five minutes chatting with my bestie or sister, yes, please! Saying yes to one more snooze button to snuggle with my cats, okay! Giving myself permission not to be perfect, not to have everything crossed off the to-do list, not to have the right answer actually put my body at ease.

I talk to women every day who want to know what one thing they could do to help with the pain of endometriosis. There isn't one tip. The answer isn't about tackling the beast of endometriosis. The answer is doing small things every day to reconnect to yourself and to bring you closer to your own happiness. In practicing moving past stress, anxiety, guilt, and anger, and replacing those feelings with love, acceptance, and positivity, overwhelming feelings start to dissipate. Practicing using your voice and listening to your body on the low-hanging-fruit situations helps build your "listening muscles" for later when harder decisions come along. Before long the beast of endometriosis, or whatever you are dealing with, slowly has less of a stronghold.

Listening to your body is an acquired skill. It requires shutting off your brain and the brain's need for logic and reason. Listening to your body requires curiosity about what that tiny voice, feeling, or irritation might be trying to tell you. I began to consider what different aches, pains, and feelings might mean. The beginning of my wellness journey was the end of ignoring my body. Everything means something, and I wanted to know what.

It's easy to ignore emotional pain, resentment, guilt, and any other negative feelings and carry on with everyday life, letting other things become more important. It is easy to blame feelings on other people or the disease. It's not easy to look inward and wonder if and how our own habits and emotions contribute to health problems. We must begin considering how we deal with the stress of chronic pain and disease, as well as everyday life. Why do we feel one way or another? What thoughts, social interactions (or lack thereof), and experiences have us feeling a certain way? Being curious about ourselves starts to shift our perceptions.

Now that we are shifting, let's figure out how to move past stress and negativity and let go of trauma.

chapter 9

cleaning your mental closet

Your beliefs become your thoughts; your thoughts become your words; your words become your actions; your actions become your habits; your habits become your values; your values become your destiny.
—Mahatma Gandhi

Addressing mental patterns is like digging through your closet. The newest, nicest stuff is up front, and as you get farther back, things get older and less used. Like that little black dress you love, but when was the last time you wore it? Even if you had an opportunity to wear it again, would you pull it out or buy a new one? How about that ten-year-old pair of jeans? Or the blazer you purchased for your first big interview after college? What about those running shoes? *Oh my gosh, is that my corsage from senior prom? Wow! Who keeps that for fifteen years? What else is in here?*

When cleaning a closet there are varying degrees of intensity, from doing laundry to reorganizing, from switching seasons to sending old stuff to Goodwill. Cleaning can be quick and easy or labor intensive and exhausting. The same is true for mental housekeeping. Internal clutter can range from daily stresses to a lifetime of destructive habits. The question is, where do you start?

I started cleaning out my mental closet using tools such as journaling and reading self-help books to help shift my perspective. Heavy cleansing came in with acupuncture, kinesiology, and chiropractic. I am continually analyzing and am curious about what can be eliminated, changed, or added to my life, so I keep removing the junk and heading in the right direction. I trust that whatever issue is up is what I am supposed to deal with by moving stagnant energy and Qi, releasing fears, or acknowledging emotional struggle.

I like to think of finding my wellness path like shopping for a new pair of jeans. First, I pick an armload of jeans off the rack and head to the dressing room. I try them all on, consider each pair, walk around in them, and sit in them. Do I feel cute? Do they make my butt look big? Some pairs stick; some pairs are an instant no. I take one or two pairs home, and at home, I try them on again. I want to see how they fit with my current wardrobe. Somehow, once the thrill of shopping is over, they aren't as cute as I first thought. And that is okay. One pair gets returned. For me, peeling back the layers of physical and emotional pain was a similar process. Three steps forward, and two steps back. But all of it was progress.

Some days I felt strong and willing to keep cleaning out the closet, motivated and inspired. The next day I felt depressed about how far I still had to go. One day I laid on the acupuncture table feeling like hell and exhausted by the whole journey. I couldn't see the end result and questioned if there would be an end. If there was, in fact, a wellness "end," I was convinced it was elusive and kept moving farther away from me.

I sobbed to Christine about how I was disappointed with my current state, questioning whether I was ever going be any better. Emotions welled up in the back of my throat, and my voice shook.

"Do I have to accept that this is how life is for me?" Tears rolled down my face. She let me have my pity party.

Christine's usual silence seemed to drag on. After a while she said, "I believe you will get better. I need you to believe it, too."

Tears soaked my hair. "It's so hard." I exhaled. Frustrated, overwhelmed, and stuck with fear and anxiety, I admitted I wanted the journey to be over. I was tired of the roller coaster and tired of being tired.

She started telling me how far I had come in the last couple of years, reminiscing about all the milestones I'd passed. And I agreed. The "Meat Grinder" was gone, but I was still hormonal and tired. My back hurt. But, yes, my overall pain level had subsided. I have moments of being grateful and other moments of annoyance and irritation.

"Right now all I see is that I'm not where I want to be."

Christine took a deep breath and replied, "I need you to believe that we will get you to your end goal, even if we have road blocks and course corrections, your wellness destination is real and attainable."

To be at ease with the current roadblock was difficult. I was tired of roadblocks! It sucked to be in the middle of another "growth opportunity." I felt like I had taken forty-one steps forward and forty steps back. Who cares if its still one giant step forward! As I felt myself slipping down the rabbit hole of despair, I reminded myself to trust my body and to trust the timing of the Universe. I took a couple deep breaths and allowed my body to relax. That's when I recognized the gremlins of fear trying to hold me back.

As my wellness journey progressed, I was elated when things were going well and depressed when they weren't. Learning to deal with my own expectations for wellness was tough. The highs of feeling joyous, healthy, and happy were really high. But when it didn't last, I felt like a rug was pulled out from under me. And the tough times became exponentially upsetting.

That day with Christine I learned the art of managing expectations. I was raised with high expectations and found it unacceptable not to meet those expectations. I still hold myself accountable, but I have shifted my mindset from expectations to goals. This shift allowed me to quit seeing roadblocks as the end of the world, and start seeing them as opportunities for beautifully unplanned detours.

This realization prompted me to get to work analyzing the things that brought on irritation or that seemed to run over and over in my mind. I didn't journal the ins and outs of every day or the rundown of events; I journaled to discover myself and the layers of hurt. Journaling helped me learn why certain situations might bother me. Some of my favorite questions are:

- What messages do you tell yourself throughout the day?
- What do the gremlins sound like?
- What is it I am holding onto that is strangling me? What do I need to acknowledge so I can let go?
- Why did this person affect me in one way or another? Why is my reaction so severe? What thoughts did I immediately have? Are there patterns in my reactions? Where in my body did I feel the reactions?
- Why did today's activities bring me feelings of guilt or anger? What was it about a certain situation that brought on aggravation?
- Is there something playing over and over in my mind that I need to get rid of?
- What is the lesson to learn here?
- If something went well, I'd ask, how can I duplicate the positive, happy feelings so I can experience it more often?

Journaling helps get the thoughts out of my head. Analyzing words on paper, rather than thoughts in my head, separates the situation from my experience. Using the information helps me to work through my emotions and identify what needs attention next. By being curious, I started to see patterns within my breakdowns and distress. As I recognized and understood my reactions, my anxiety levels dropped and I was able to bounce back faster. The faster I could recognize an emotional downward spiral, the faster I could work through the issue, therefore breaking the cycle of stress and pain.

Early on some of the easiest shifts were lifestyle changes such as eliminating fast food, sugar, and over-exercising. These simple behaviors were connected to destructive mental patterns. For example, hating my body showed up in my diet by abusing junk food and sugar. Rejecting femininity showed up by over-exercising to reduce body fat and eliminate curves and softness in my figure.

How we treat our environment, show up in relationships, and treat our bodies is all a reflection of our inner thoughts. This was a radical idea for me, yet it was so influential! Letting go of seemingly insignificant lifestyle habits was actually helping me clear my mental closet and connect to my emotional body.

Consider this: what if letting go of the crud that lives in the dark shadows is the way to stop the cycle of hurtful mental patterns and create a new reality? What if you didn't have to live life proving your parents wrong? Or doing the opposite of your sister in order to stand out? What if the rebellion you started in high school could be over? Do you even remember what you were rebelling against anyway? Every moment of every day we can choose to start new. We choose our thoughts, and our current thoughts create our future reality—I had never heard of such a thing until my healing journey began. Once I realized many people believe that and live this way, I felt motivated and empowered.

In my quest to understand my emotional body and inner wisdom, I was attracted to the world of self-help. Over the years, several healers have emerged with interpretations for bodily aches, pains, and diseases. Louise Hay is the pioneer in finding mental causes for physical illness and creating positive affirmations to replace old thought patterns. In her book, *Heal Your Body,* she lists areas of the body, common ailments, and their probable causes, as well as new thought patterns for beginning to let go of such issues. The key here is that we can listen to our bodies and use the signs to discover what negative messages need to be addressed.

By using Louise Hay's list, I've been able to keep tabs on the gremlins. For example, years ago I would consistently come down with nasty sinus infections. According to Hay's list, sinus problems show irritation with someone close. I could take this information to the kinesiologist and work through the layers of my irritation. I took this approach even deeper and looked at my menstrual pain. Hay suggests my body is trying to tell me to look at guilt, fear, or rejection around femininity and being a woman. Well, doesn't that make sense for me? Again, this could mean a lot of different things to a lot of different women, but for me it made sense to look at my severe dislike for my reproductive organs. After witnessing how much my thoughts and beliefs affected my body, I could see the vicious cycle between endometriosis causing pain, anger, and hate, and these negative feelings manifesting as more pain and discomfort.

Here is a recent discovery for me and an example of how listening to your body can be used for everyday situations: I work from home and lately have been increasingly agitated when my husband, Aaron, comes home from work. It makes no sense—I should be happy to see my husband, right? He walks in the front door, comes back to the office, and gives me a kiss. We then talk about our days, figure out what we are doing for dinner, and discuss any other plans for the evening. However, recently, I'd rather be left alone. I'd get moody and agitated and find something to blame him for.

As I journaled about it, I wrote, "How would he like it if I unexpectedly showed up at his office at 3:00 in the afternoon expecting him to drop everything to entertain me?" The statement stopped me in my tracks and made me realize he gets to choose when he is finished working for the day. On his short drive home, he decompresses and transitions into home life. I, on the other hand, felt interrupted and a loss of power around when I finish work, which caused resentment. As Aaron and I discussed how I felt, we decided that when he comes home, although I am excited to see him and want to say hi, I need twenty to thirty minutes to finish my work. I get to choose when I am done working. It's a win-win situation. I was able to express myself, and he understands what's happening for me. Everyone is happy!

Now, does that have anything to do directly with chronic pain and endometriosis? Not on the surface. However, within the practice of recognizing, addressing, and giving voice to my emotional body, I'm gaining confidence for when complicated chronic pain and endometriosis issues arise. Most importantly, this practice helps me recognize tension and thus manage stress. The sooner I recognize negative patterns, stress, and tension, the less likely those will get stuck in my body and manifest as pain.

———•———

Stress and gremlins are best friends; activating stress gives the gremlins the energy to ransack our mental closets. When I'm stressed, everything seems difficult, complicated, and irritating. Now, living from a place of choosing to do what's best for my body and my health, I know a heightened state of stress doesn't support an ability to react well to tense situations. Our bodies can only take so much.

There is a wonderful analogy out there called *The Spoon Theory* by Christine Miserandino.[2] The story began as Christine, who has been diagnosed with lupus, explains how living with a chronic disease is about making choices about where to spend daily energy. In an attempt to explain her situation, she gave a friend a handful of spoons to represent her limited energy resources. Christine explained that every activity costs a spoon, and when your spoons run out for the day, so does your energy and ability to complete tasks. Getting dressed costs a spoon, driving costs a spoon, calling mom costs a spoon, being at work or school costs several spoons, and so on.

---

[2] Miserandino, Christine, "The Spoon Theory", http://www.butyoudont looksick.com/articles/written-by-christine/the-spoon-theory/

Many invisible-illness communities have adopted this spoon analogy. It is a great way to not only think about energy reserves but also about stress management. When 3:00 p.m. rolls around and you have two spoons left, what do you do? What activities do you choose? The spoon analogy helps others understand how someone with a chronic illness has to consider activities from day to day—and that when energy is gone, it is gone. Chronic pain and illness force you to prioritize choices about whether to cook or clean, work or play, etc. A vital part of healing is understanding *your* body and respecting its limits. Depleting energy reserves is directly related to your ability to heal and deal with day-to-day stress. For me, depleting energy reserves had been my way of life.

One of the causes of my stress came from how the disease affected my quality of life. I expected myself to be like everyone else. And when I fell short, I felt alone and isolated. Endometriosis and pain flare-ups were activated and intensified by stress and discontentment, among other things.

For example, every month my menstrual cycle inflicted a roller coaster of emotions. I had expectations that my life and period should look as other women's appeared—you know, calm, cool, and collected, not the psycho bitch on a wild roller coaster ride. I poured all my energy into making sure psycho bitch wouldn't happen. Because birth control perfectly regulated my cycle to twenty-eight days, I could look ahead in my calendar and know where stress points were going to be. Helpful for planning purposes? Maybe. Strengthening my beliefs that my period only brings wretched pain, anger, and disappointment? You bet. I knew when the first and last day of my period would be. I knew when ovulation would start. I knew how many days of pain were upon me. With almost two decades of proof, why would this month or next month or any month be any different? With all the pain and exhaustion looming in the future, I had to take care of growing to-do lists right away, or I wouldn't get to it for at least a week—which I viewed as unacceptable!

Yet again, my period ruled my life, reinforcing anxiety for next month. Without fail, compounding stress, anxiety, and disappointment layered on and added to my discomfort. I missed my best friend's thirtieth birthday party. I'd spent Thanksgiving in bed. I'd said no to countless social gatherings, and Aaron had said "hello" for me, apologizing for my absence more times than I could count. Fear and anxiety around my period was just about as bad as my actual period.

I could clearly see making undesirable situations "bad" was creating stress and tension. Recognizing the vicious cycle was no longer an intellectual thought, I was witnessing the connection. Daily emotional stresses were causing flare-ups and tension within my body, leading to pain. The pain caused discontentment and anxiety, which created emotional stress. I felt like a rat in a wheel, stuck and frustrated.

The more I learned about how important managing stress is to healing, the more interested I became in mastering the art of listening to my emotions. Mastering (not eliminating) emotions for period-anxiety looked like digging through my mental closet and getting rid of a few "T-shirts" I was used to wearing. A few of my favorite graphic T's read:

- *Let's all pretend I'm fine.*
- *Hi! I'm the broken girl, you know, the one that's always bailing on commitments.*
- *My period is coming! My period is coming! My period is coming! It should be here in about five days.*

Those t-shirts had to go! I've replaced them with these:

- *Listen to your body.*
- *My sensitive body is powerful.*

75

Like anything else, when I saw a direct correlation and immediate improvement, I wanted to continue to replicate the positive results. Recognizing and eliminating stressors helped me feel at ease and keep negativity at bay.

Most mental housekeeping is getting rid of old, unwanted crud, and kicking out the gremlins. There are also a lot of items I could have used more of, like white t-shirts, classic blazers, or a variety of emotions. For the longest time, I operated from a place of *good or bad, angry or not angry, in pain or not in pain*. This duality was doing me no good. Did you know you can have more than two feelings about any given topic? I needed some serious expansion in this department.

At my monthly kinesiology sessions, we worked through recognizing (for the particular topic my body presented) whether I needed to add to my closet (learning) or empty the closet (letting go). And many times, it was both. Letting go of an old unhelpful pattern and replacing that space with positive affirmations, gratitude, love, and acceptance.

Acknowledging negative emotions is key. Historically, if I felt scared, apprehensive, or frightened, I would make myself wrong and implement some fear-based short-term avoidance mechanism. Making it okay to experience negative emotions was new and interesting. The idea to experience hurt, acknowledge that it exists, and then be able to let it go sounded counter-intuitive. Somehow naming the elephant in the room turned him into a mouse. It is quite liberating. Now I know that acknowledging my negative feelings, accepting them as a part of me, and loving myself through them is the only way to really let them go. Ignoring ugly feelings never made them go away. They just festered like a nasty skin infection until I had no other choice but to deal with them. Holding onto negative events, thoughts, and opinions creates dis-stress, dis-trust, and dis-ease in the body.

With help from kinesiology and acupuncture, emotional heaviness started lifting. Releasing heavy emotions made room for joy and happiness to take up residence where the gremlins used to camp out. Just as continued negativity can drain us and lead to more serious conditions, joy, on the other hand, can strengthen our ability to love and accept ourselves.

Endometriosis and chronic pain inherently provided continued hurtful experiences. So accepting myself, my history with endometriosis, and eliminating isolation around the disease also meant making it safe for me to revisit memories. Because I spent the majority of my life separating endometriosis as an undesired part of me, reconnecting meant remembering. Much of the treatment of endometriosis was traumatic, and I was scared to remember. We did a lot of work around being able to recollect fifteen years with endometriosis and chronic pain without having to relive it all. My kinesiologist helped me trust that I was in a different place now and had the capability to handle discussing traumatic situations, whereas in the past I did not. I had to trust in the holistic healing work we'd done. We strengthened emotional wires to allow me not only to see my past, but also to understand and learn from every experience.

Mental housekeeping is a crucial component of healing and maintaining wellness. Continually cleaning out my mental closet and adding small, yet positive, lifestyle changes allowed me to see improvement. Over time the modifications and actions added up to significant lasting transformation.

The more I learned, the more I understood that the Universe sends the same mental exam over and over until you, the true you, learns it. When we truly hear and integrate lessons into our whole selves, the issues stop resurfacing. And we get to grow and heal.

chapter 10

money & worth

*Money in and of itself is nothing. It's what money represents
that makes the whole shebang a little complex.*
–Kate Northrup, Money, a Love Story

was raised in a hard-working Midwestern family. You work, and
you save. You do not spend money on yourself unless you absolutely
have no other choice. Money is security, so you don't want to spend
it and have nothing to show for it later.

The topic of money causes stress for a lot of people for myriad
reasons. Trying to deal with health issues, any perceived lack of
available money, or spending money for wellness can cause anxiety
and helplessness. The topic of money and my wellness oozed with
guilt and self-worth issues.

Crunch time came on a Thursday in August 2008. That
afternoon, I was called into my boss's office. I lost my job—and my
insurance. Being laid off was not a huge surprise. The economy
was tanking, and the bottom fell out of the construction and
architecture industry. Many of my interior design friends were
facing job loss. Being so sick, I had already cut back to a thirty-
hour workweek, if you could even call it that. Plus, as I previously
mentioned, I wasn't exactly a model employee around this time.

Losing my job was one thing. Losing my all-important
insurance was devastating. Four days prior, Aaron started a new

job where he had a waiting period to be covered by the new company's insurance. In 2008 there was a sixty-three-day look-back period when insurance companies did not have to cover pre-existing conditions. With a laparoscopy surgery nine months prior, numerous endometriosis specialists, and pelvic pain physical therapy appointments, I had a clear pre-existing condition.

Facing a loss of income and the possibility of no insurance, my stress level shot to an all-time high. I believed there was no way we could afford any of my treatments. As if I needed another excuse for not making myself and my health a priority, now I had financial stress. It ended up that Aaron's insurance kicked in just in time, and I was covered. The days of waiting to know what was going to happen, however, were excruciating. I'm sure I gave myself hives and twitchy eyes.

Even with insurance, the chance of getting endometriosis treatments covered wasn't necessarily guaranteed. Insurance companies classified endometriosis as a fertility, or "nonmedical," issue. And although major improvements in their willingness to pay for these "nonmedical" related issues have vastly improved since I was first diagnosed in 1995, coverage was never guaranteed. I already knew my endometriosis specialist at the time was expensive and rarely covered by insurance. Phone calls alone for prescription refills cost hundreds of dollars. Don't even get me started on the cost of additional internal ultrasounds to "double-check" for new cysts. I had to beg the receptionist to *please* code my visits as non-fertility to have any chance of insurance helping out. So I was definitely freaking out about medical bills and not having a job. I didn't know how we were going to get through it.

Aaron was the one who suggested that maybe the time off from work would be a blessing. *A blessing? How are we going to pay for all of my medical bills?* At $1,500 a month in post-insured medical expenses, I was convinced we couldn't sustain it for long. We were going to be broke, and it would be all my fault.

In October 2008, I had started seeing Christine for acupuncture.

And although seeing her was a wonderful gift, it was yet another line item on the budget. Something had to give. Money was flying out the door, and I was doing nothing in the way of contributing. I wasn't working, and I was spending all the money on myself. As the budget nerd in the family, my head was about to explode. Can you feel guilt and anxiety rising?

Looking back, I see that my mindset made no sense. I was sicker than ever. I had been "given" time off to take care of myself, yet I was pissed off and stressed out because of it. I was convinced we were going to have no money, safety, or security.

At the time, I was going to acupuncture and physical therapy once a week and kinesiology and massage once a month. All of this was in addition to seeing specialist after specialist and filling ever-increasing prescriptions. As I sat in front of the computer paying bills and reconciling the checkbook, I was in tears. *Why can't I just be better? When am I going to be back to normal? I can't do this anymore. We can't afford any of this.* In truth, subconsciously, I felt unworthy of the expense.

One night I announced I was going to quit massage and physical therapy, and limit acupuncture appointments, saying, "We can't afford it anymore." Aaron asked why, commenting that they all seemed to be helping. And they were. But those appointments represented over $900 a month. Saying the total out loud made me feel sick.

Aaron looked me straight in the eyes and said, "So what. What do we work for if we can't take care of you?" At first I tried to argue that cutting therapy costs is better for our household, but then I just sat there. I'd never thought of it like that. In that moment, I'd never felt more loved. He hugged me and said, "We will do whatever it takes to get you back to being you." He thought I was worth the expense.

That day Aaron reminded me that if we really wanted to, we could choose to find the money for me to get well. We could find a way to rearrange our priorities. In other words, lattes, upgraded cable TV and HD sports packages, name brand designer clothing, and dinners out had to go. He said those things are not priorities when your wife doesn't get out of bed. This concept was clear for him—but guilt-ridden for me.

It was strange that I could easily rearrange the budget to save for a trip to London to see my sister, or for the beautiful new car we'd been drooling over, but I struggled to make myself a priority. Shifting importance toward myself. It felt selfish. Valuing myself and letting our bank account reflect this shift was hard. When I thought about it in terms of trading an item for my health, then it became clear to me.

Ever experience that? Could you trade a monthly pedicure for reiki or trigger point massage? What about giving up two lattes a week for a monthly acupuncture appointment?

I understand how stressful it is to feel like all the household money is being spent on healthcare and to wish that you could use money for fun things like vacations or new outfits from Target. I also understand feeling like some treatments are out of reach because either insurance won't cover them, or they are too expensive. It was a powerful exercise for Aaron and me to work through our priorities, shift the flow of money, and work through our beliefs about it. We came up with a unified view so money didn't rule our decisions. It changed our mindset from *I can't; we can't afford it* to *If we really wanted to, we could choose to spend our money on my health.* As healing became a priority, it was easy to cut unnecessary items out of our life. Our life became simpler and more focused. Not only did I feel power within our choices and power over the bank account, but I also began to feel that I was worth it.

When it came to spending, one aspect I had to reconsider was how we budgeted for food. Prior to alternative healing, I had a pretty solid habit of fast food and junk food. When I would (rarely) grocery shop, I would buy food that was cheap and easy to prepare. I hate cooking. I never really paid attention to ingredients, preservatives, or whether an item was certified organic. I would never consider paying more for an item simply because I thought its ingredients were better for me. After my acupuncturist put me through a cleanse to rid my body of junk, I had to replace the junk food habit with clean eating. We eliminated sugar, processed foods, preservatives, and hormones. I became a label reader and a food snob. I altered the way we shopped, cooked, and made choices about food. Clean eating means cooking with *real* ingredients. No fake butter created from chemicals. No "granola bars" coated in high fructose corn syrup. No yogurt with aspartame.

Although the cost of changing my diet initially gave me sticker shock, I could feel the difference in my body. I'd honestly never done a cleanse before. It was nothing fancy, just eliminating bad food and reintroducing real food. I felt energized and full, as in full of life instead of stuffed and bloated. I felt nourished. I felt good with good food and like crap with crappy food. With feeling better a priority, we made room in the budget for clean food and never looked back.

Money is a difficult topic with plenty of beliefs, emotions, and influences attached. A million money gurus out there have thousands of opinions about what you should or shouldn't be doing with money. A couple of ideas I have gravitated toward are from Dave Ramsey and Kate Northrup. Dave Ramsey believes that personal finances are *personal*. There is no fancy, sophisticated, mathematical formula that is going to ease money stress. The only way to control finances is to control the person in the mirror. Kate Northrup encourages us to align spending habits with our core beliefs. Choose to spend on what helps us grow and expand with our personal beliefs vs. unconsciously spending on items that only support short-term satisfaction. How fitting—managing money was another layer of managing stress and connecting to my inner self.

chapter 11

outside stress

Don't let the noise of other people's opinion drown out your inner voice.
—Steve Jobs

ealing with outside stresses isn't actually about the other person. At the core of the issue, it has nothing to do with someone else. Other people simply act as a mirror of our own beliefs. Ever notice judgments and criticism in areas where we are confident or grounded seem to roll right past us? The difficult part is that opinions, judgments, and criticisms hurt when it reflects what we feel (consciously or unconsciously) about ourselves. Any speck of uncertainty within us leaves room for gremlins of stress and shame to creep in and take over, often leaving room for others to interject their opinions.

I often felt severely hurt by others' comments (on many subjects) and used to think other people were insensitive, rude, or mean. Now I know the hurt was simply pointing me in the direction of my own negative thoughts and beliefs. The ability to distinguish insecurities and internal conflict was the first step to let outside stress roll past me. Being grounded meant the noise of others no longer took hold of my emotions.

Outside stress seemed to stick the most when it pertained to my healthcare choices, setting boundaries, shifting relationships, and my ability to bear children. Back when I was really sick, I would discuss treatments with everyone. Navigating through the best treatment options while heavily medicated was difficult, so I appreciated the input. I honestly didn't know what was best for me, so I'd seek advice. Discussing a situation and decision was how I sorted out my thoughts, especially since I was diagnosed so young. I had rarely made my own healthcare decisions. This made sense as a teenager, but as I grew into adulthood, I struggled with the transition of decisions becoming truly mine. I placed more importance on the opinions of others than I did on my own. It was tough to let go of needing my parents' or anyone else's input. It was even harder to believe I was in control of my health and my path to wellness.

For someone whose body is incredibly sensitive, stress easily activates pain. I had enough to work through on my own, adding other people's opinions or stresses to the equation was just too much.

When I chose to turn to alternative ways of healing, I was excited to share about my new path. For the first time, I was headed in the right direction. As my therapies became increasingly alternative and holistic, I began to believe and witness that any emotional discomfort or negative thoughts could manifest physically. However, for those closest to me, the idea was by far the craziest thing they'd ever heard. When I spoke about the therapies that were helping me most, I felt like people thought, *What a weirdo,* and looked at me like I had four heads. *Does she believe this kinesiology stuff? Really—changing thought patterns and releasing past stress is going to ease her pain? Think positive and you shall heal? Yeah right!*

No one understood me because no one had been exposed to such ideas. I was blazing a new trail, which sounds so romantic and courageous. But in reality, it felt unfamiliar, scary, and isolating. My people-pleasing self's need to fit in felt exposed and uncomfortable.

At first, I was self-conscious and unsure about how to express myself. My lack of confidence left room for others to pick apart my "weird" methods. Eventually I stopped sharing, not from a place of defeat, but from a place of strength.

I had to take a break from sharing and first find healing. This gave evidence to my methods instead of a mere hypothesis. Those around me could see improvement and soon had questions about what I was up to. With evidence of a symptom-free life, my confidence grew. I witnessed my body improving. I saw real growth and change. I no longer felt I had to defend myself or stand up to others' judgments. I was healing and connecting to my true self, so my sharing came across as a statement, not a question. Grounded and rooted within my body, I found that unconditional love for myself about my chosen treatment methods became stronger, and the vice grip of other people's opinions loosened.

Doesn't that sound great? Find self-love and compassion, then the words of others simply lose their power. It is that simple—and it isn't. The method is simple; the journey is not.

It took me a long time to realize that most people give their opinions based on their own reality. They can only look at my situation through the filter of their own experience. Their feedback tells more about *them* than it does about *me*. We all filter "what's best" through our own experience, culture, upbringing, influences, and imprinting. And yes, others' ideas and opinions help us see outside our own box—whether we agree, there is always a lesson. My mistake is that I long forgot that I might have ideas and opinions for myself. What a concept! I let others' thoughts steamroll my own. This is why listening to *your* body and the quietest parts of yourself is so important.

How do you start shifting value from outside opinions to internal wisdom? That was a tough question for me. Values are much closer to the core of us (if you recall the diagram in chapter five, outside stress is an outer layer) and harder to change. I decided to do what was easiest to alleviate outside stress in the moment: Set some boundaries.

One of the first boundaries I had to set with my family was that we would only talk about my health if I brought it up. Just like repeating myself with nurses and doctors, continually answering questions about pain and symptoms only reminded me and reinforced how crappy I felt. Those closest to me cared about my well-being, but continual discussion about symptoms only kept them in the forefront of my life and made me irritable. Anxiety rose when my mom called, and then I'd be cranky and testy with all the questions. It wasn't fair to her or to anyone else. In the long run, asking my loved ones to stop inquiring about endometriosis symptoms and pain was the best for me. By setting boundaries, I got to be in control and choose the timing of discussions about my health.

Many of my relationships changed because of the boundaries. Those who truly loved me loved me more as I blossomed. Letting go of what others thought and becoming authentically me allowed my relationships to deepen and strengthen. Even my marriage grew in ways I never imagined. Aaron became a supportive sounding board for my frightened internal voice. My best friend became even more of a best friend. My relationship with my family went through some tough times but now couldn't be better. Some friends dropped off, and that it is okay. Most importantly, love for myself grew.

We all need input from friends and family. I am not suggesting ignoring other people. There is much to learn from hearing others' perspectives and hearing our own perspective within different conversations. Conversations bring up ideas we may never have thought about before, and whether the other person provides criticism or questions, the feedback is invaluable. Conversations can make us think in ways we wouldn't necessarily on our own. The question becomes, "can we assess what's valuable and what's not while standing in our inner wisdom." For a long time, all I could hear was criticism. I had placed too much value on deciding whether I was right or wrong depending on others' ideas.

Throughout my life, questions about having children have been the most problematic. Early on in my diagnosis, doctors questioned whether I would be able to have children, which I largely ignored. As a teenager, the discussion didn't particularly interest me. Once I was out of college and married, however, inquiries about our plans for a family increased. After our wedding, our answer was that we were on the "five-year plan," which seemed to suffice. And to be honest, it was the truth. We always felt like adding children to our relationship was something to handle at a later date. However, as the "five-year plan" expired, questions regarding having a family began to really pile on. By the time our late twenties rolled around, those closest to us wanted to know when they could expect little ones running around.

I didn't know the answer, and I definitely didn't know how to deal with the pressure. From family to bosses and random acquaintances, everyone seemed to have ideas about having babies, especially in our hometown in Nebraska.

At a bar over the holidays, I found myself talking to a girl from high school. Although we were friends years ago, college and life had put some distance between us. As we chatted she commented, "Now that you and Aaron are married, I bet you can't wait for a minivan full of kids?"

I promptly answered with "Gawd, no!"

As I was about to launch into how awful that sounded, she excitedly told me how she was dreaming of four kids, soccer games, and dance recitals. To be honest, I'd literally never had those thoughts. In college I remember having conversations with girlfriends about "never" having kids. But as more and more of our friends started having families, my opinion became less and less popular until I realized I was alone in the idea. Then I began to feel like something was wrong with me. Something changed for our friends that didn't change for me. I mean, at thirty, I should have been having maternal thoughts, right? Some sort of feeling? Anything? But nothing. Disney movies, daycare, and diapers became the topic of conversation, and I had nothing to add. Not until my nephew was born could I add anything valuable to a conversation about teething. My connection to my friends suffered.

The kiddo question affected me for years. A woman I worked with once asked when we were going to have kids. At the time, I was inching toward the idea that maybe having children wasn't in the cards for me. I answered that I wasn't sure we were going to. Her response will always be one of my favorites: "Don't you think it is selfish to not have children?" Wow! What do you say to that one? I just shrugged my shoulders but a wave of guilt washed over my body. I had never thought of the choice as being selfish. I'd rather be honest with myself than to have children out of pressure and obligation. How awful would it be for a child to grow up in a home where Mom was resentful?

With all these kiddo questions swirling around, I struggled to express myself. I tried everything. "I don't know" never seemed to satisfy; it was usually followed by a barrage of suggestions and loaded opinions. For a while I tried an undertone of revenge; in other words, you made me feel badly about myself, and I'd do the same to you. I would answer with, "Oh, you didn't know, I was diagnosed with a painful reproductive disease at age fourteen. I can't have kids." (Truthfully, I don't know whether my body is able to have children or not). Although the "I can't" answer usually quieted the other person, I spoke it out of anger and spite, and I still felt guilty. I even tried jokingly answering with, "No kids for us!" However, I'd usually awkwardly over-explain. Plus, any uncertainty on my part left space for someone else to unload his or her thoughts. Until I found my truth, I continued to struggle.

One year over Thanksgiving, one of my aunts inquired about the status of our child production, to which I answered with my usual, "I don't know. Haven't really thought about it." She then informed me that my clock was ticking, "Your eggs are going to dry up!" I wasn't even thirty at the time. It felt like a drive-by shooting. It happened so fast, I was without words, and then it was over. I felt like crap about myself but had to pull myself together to make it through the rest of Thanksgiving.

Some of the most hurtful questions came from close family. For quite a few years, I needed a therapy sandwich around going home to Nebraska: a session before heading home to prepare myself and a session immediately after returning to let go of negativity. Since I was self-conscious in the first place, it was easy to take on other people's ideas about what I should or shouldn't be doing with my life. Then, subsequently, I'd feel bad because I didn't "measure up" to others' opinions. I was stuck in that vicious cycle for far too long!

One weekend, I was asked four times when a grandbaby would be added to the family. I felt ashamed for not knowing the answer and experienced immense guilt that, as badly as this person wanted a grandbaby, it wouldn't be coming from me. On one hand, I felt that it was my choice, my body, and my life. On the other hand, I felt the weight of "wrecking" another person's dream. Anger built inside of me, and as much as I tried to avoid the question or cover my emotion with sarcasm, my insecurity and shame was crippling. My body was throbbing, my head pounding, and my eyes twitching as I tried to hold back an explosion of angry tears.

Although Aaron overheard the comments, they never bothered him. I couldn't understand why I was the only one upset. *It was bullshit! Did he hear that comment? Why didn't he care? Wasn't all the harassment pissing him off? Couldn't he see the questions were ripping me apart? Why was I the one fronting the answers?*

I broke down crying to Aaron at the end of the weekend about how it's nobody's f---ing business whether we have kids. I couldn't deal with my own internal conflict, outside pressure, and feeling like I didn't have a partner to support me. Not until I used these words did Aaron understand that outside opinions were not "just questions." Of course, he didn't get it; no was asking him about being a dad. And he didn't have major internal conflict about the topic, so the opinions just rolled off him. Fortunately, Aaron was able to understand my perspective and grasp the depth of my struggle. As tears, snot, and sweat poured out of me, Aaron told me he'd take care of it. That night he sat down individually with our families, taking the brunt of their questions, thoughts, and opinions. With expectations and pressures eliminated, I could feel at ease, supported, and safe to make the best decision for me, and for us.

Since we are talking about it, here are some of my favorite outside stress comments. I couldn't help but include them:

- "I have a great fertility doctor, you should see him." *Yes, that would be great if I were actually trying to be pregnant, but I'm not.*
- "Why don't you have kids yet? You'd make the cutest kids." *I do appreciate the compliments. But cuteness is not a reason to procreate.*
- "Don't you want to provide your husband with offspring." *Oh, the guilt! Did you even ask if my husband wants to be a dad?*
- "If you cannot have kids, will you adopt? How do you love a child that is not your own?" *Wow, really?*

The biggest lesson I've learned is that an opinion is just an opinion. While I worked through my own issues, it was important to differentiate between drive-by conversations and helpful ones. I've learned to "bobblehead" my way through an awful conversation. Nod and smile, and then let it go. For people who do not understand what I've gone through, or been through a significant struggle or transformation of their own, I've decided their opinions aren't useful to me anyway. A good friend of mine once said, "If you haven't walked through the valley of shit, you do not get to comment on my journey through the valley of shit." Amen, sister!

Whatever your outside stressors are, until you find inner peace, the opinions, criticisms, and judgments of others will have the upper hand. Feedback tells more about the person giving than receiving. Once an awful conversation is over, the most important thing is to not make the opinion mean anything about you personally. Others' opinions mean more about them than they do about you.

Even though the majority of exterior influences can easily pile on, their stress can be easier to recognize because they are on the surface level. For me, a bit of insulation from the noise did a lot of good. I'm not suggesting to forever live in a bubble. Just as a broken leg needs a cast and some rest, emotional healing could use a shield from stress and some rest from pain. A little break from outside stresses so I could look inward and grow stronger benefited everyone in the long run.

It is possible to be confident in who we are in some areas of life yet feel vulnerable and unsure in other areas. We have to find people who support us and ask questions that connect us to our inner wisdom so we can discover what is best for us. Navigating through relationships and interactions with other people can be difficult, but it provides an opportunity to be authentic. In choosing to be authentic, we find unconditional self-love. As our confidence and authenticity grows, we are able to differentiate between our own thoughts and the opinions of others. We can more quickly move past the issue, not letting it affect our bodies and minds.

As you dig through layers of pain and healing, you get to discover yourself. You get to control outside stresses and stop being affected by the opinions of others. You become clear about what is right for you and find confidence to speak your truth. And that will always bring you one step closer to listening to your body and reconnecting to inner wisdom.

chapter 12

shameful identities

"Nothing to hold on to" is the root of happiness.
– Pema Chödrön, The Places That Scare Us

My brain produces 10,000 thoughts a minute. For much of my life, I considered most of those thoughts to be the truth.

Our brains have two ways of managing information: the conscious mind and the subconscious mind. The conscious mind is analytical. It judges the world around us, filtering information as right, wrong, or otherwise. It is our intellect and retains all the information from places like geography class, the boss's to-do list, and the family's weekly schedule. This part of our brain evolves slowly over the first decade of life, and as we make it through puberty, our conscious mind is fully developed. My conscious mind is a chronic overachiever, rarely satisfied with current results, always pushing for more, and extremely self-critical.

The subconscious mind, on the other hand, is non-analytical, intuitive, and controls our feelings. The subconscious mind is fully developed the moment we are born, and, unlike our conscious mind, it does not differentiate between right or wrong, good or bad, true or false. As infants, toddlers, and small children, when we are learning how the world works, we believe what we are told, soak up the attitudes of those around us, pick up beliefs, and learn tools to deal with emotions. We learned some fairly hefty stuff all before the age of two! Think about how much of our thought patterns and emotional growth developed before we had any say in it.

Aren't you ready to have a say in it? What if your thoughts are not true? How the heck do you filter through all of that noise and attempt to listen to your body?

As you can imagine, our families and cultures influence our beliefs, how we feel about ourselves, and how we interact with others. It's your mom's fault you have body image issues, your dad's fault you're never satisfied, and your aunt's fault you think shopping is therapy. We've picked up all kinds of behaviors from those around us, just like they did. These flawed beliefs rule our subconscious, and our subconscious rules our life. Before you make a phone call to your mom informing her she ruined your life, know this: We have a choice in the matter. We can't blame our parents, their parents, or anyone else. Everyone is doing the best they can with the tools and knowledge they were given. It is our own fault if we continually choose to run the script of our past.

Few of us question these deeply ingrained thoughts and beliefs. Developmentally speaking, sometime in our mid-twenties is when most adults unhook from their parent's views. This doesn't necessarily mean we act any differently from the first twenty years of imprinting; it just means we have the ability to choose differently. Much of the learning we do as adults is actually unlearning what we picked up in childhood and replacing it with information and tools that fit us now. But again, this is a choice. So many adults do not make the choice to make major changes—until something forces us to do so.

For me, the role for women was defined by progress toward motherhood and the ability to run a household. In my mid-twenties, my major struggles revolved around these learned gender roles. My influences and imprinting about being a woman were very traditional, and I hated it. Rejection of these gender roles and dislike for my "broken" female parts caused major internal conflict. My own thoughts and beliefs toward being a woman and a mother did not align with what I was taught. I was confused, ashamed, and upset. Even worse, I didn't have the tools to deal with confusing emotions. I felt like I didn't fit in, like there was something wrong with me.

According to Brené Brown, a researcher at the University of Houston, shame starts in the subconscious mind. Shame is a painful emotion caused by consciousness of guilt, shortcoming, or impropriety. If you think back to the Pain Layers Diagram and the idea that our physical and emotional bodies are like onions, we can place shame right on top of negative thoughts and beliefs. And just like outside stresses, shame takes place between people and is all about perceptions.

Shame can be activated as we interact with other people, no matter what the relationship is like. Within relationships and conversations with other people, our reactions reveal where we carry shame. Shame makes us feel like we are different and the only ones who have ever felt this way. However, if we can find the courage to share our experiences, we have an opportunity to connect with our true selves and to those around us. What I love about Brown's work is her acknowledgement that shame happens between people and is healed between people.

Shame is what I call a bottom layer emotion. At first glance, our response to a shameful event usually comes out as anger, hurt, or confusion. If you can dig into your feelings, under any reactionary blameful anger is a core feeling that sounds something like *I'm not enough. I am not a good enough wife. My ideas aren't good enough to share with the world. I'm not in good enough shape to run a 5K . . .* You get the point. Unwanted subconscious beliefs are often the root of shame reactions.

Shame kicks in when, deep down, raw emotions are activated. These raw emotions can come to the surface in a split second, which can be confusing. No one wants to feel embarrassed and isolated and vulnerable, so our natural response is to get rid of it. We use every trick in the book to run, hide, cover up, and pretend shame is not there.

As I think back throughout the first three decades of my life, and specifically to how I dealt with endometriosis and chronic pain, shame ran my life. I tried to insulate myself from emotional hurt so I wouldn't feel shame or any other awful feeling. Ugly feelings meant stress, which meant tension, which meant pain. So let's just avoid this all together, shall we?

Shame is such a destructive emotion because we get stuck in a vicious cycle of questioning who we are and feeling like "bad" people. Shame causes us to shrink and robs us of being authentic. The good news is, we can learn to recognize shame and let go before it takes over and gets stuck in our bodies.

The most influential resource for me about shame is Brené Brown's book *I Thought It Was Just Me*. Brown, along with Dr. Linda Hartling, suggests there are three ways we protect ourselves from shame. We either move away from the situation by avoiding it, move toward the situation by seeking approval, or move against the situation by wanting to make the other person feel badly or by seeking revenge. We may act differently in different situations.

Their exercise about shame triggers and unwanted identities hit home for me, uncovering a wealth of information. Brown gives categories that carry the most shame: appearance and body image, motherhood, family, parenting, money, work, mental and physical health, sex, aging, religion, being labeled, speaking out, and surviving trauma. She then prompts her readers to write the following: "When it comes to [insert category], I do not want to be perceived as [fill in blank]. I want to be perceived as [fill in blank]." I did this exercise for each category. For the surviving trauma category, I wrote, "I do not want to be perceived as weak, less able, broken, or damaged. On the flip side, I do want to be perceived as having courage, changing the world, helping women, and being strong." This exercise allowed me to visually see what I emotionally felt in moments of shame and connect the internal wires of my emotions and pain.

Now when I feel the gut-wrenching sensation of shame, I can

recall this list and catch myself in the shame spiral. Instead of harboring resentment, spewing ugliness, or running the internal highlight reel of the event, I recognize my feelings. Acknowledging shame breaks the cycle. Then I can be on my way to letting go.

Years ago one shame trigger was when people would say to me, "I can tell you aren't feeling well." I'd feel the wave of paralysis come over me. I didn't want to be perceived as broken. The comment felt like a congratulatory gesture to themselves rather than a way to connect with me. I'm sure other people meant something more along the lines of, "I am sorry you aren't feeling well. You should go home and take care of yourself." I understand trying to be helpful or empathetic, which is nice. But I could only hear, "Wow, you look like shit." And when it took all my energy to get out of bed, the comment never landed well. My way of dealing with these comments was to seek approval by urging the other person to believe I was fine. But I distanced myself from that person, thinking, *If I never have to be in this person's presence again, we won't have to talk about how I am feeling.*

Severe shame responses are visceral. I remember feeling like I was radiating heat—angry, hateful, 150-degree heat—once at a social event, when someone asked, "How have you been lately? Are you finally stable?" It should be no surprise that my head just about spun off my body. I thought to myself, *Well, I think I'm stable, am I not? You think I am not stable? Who else thinks I'm not stable? OMG, am I not stable?* I am sure the confused look on my face said it all, but the actual words out of my mouth were more like, "I don't know what you mean?" with an undertone of *you're an ass!* My psyche was thinking that crying in the bathroom for an hour and then snuggling with my cats sounded better than continuing to remain in this situation. *Thanks for ruining my next twenty-four hours while I sort through why your stupid ass pissed me off so much. By the way, can I borrow $100 to make an emergency call to my kinesiologist?*

Take a moment to think about this: When it comes to your health, how do you want to be perceived? Are there any undesirable traits you wouldn't want to be judged by? For example, I did not want anyone to think I was less capable because of endometriosis and chronic pain. Years ago when I confided in a female coworker about how I took sick days because of my period, she informed me that having your period does not deserve a sick day. I felt like she looked down on me and judged me as weak: *You should suck it up and get to work.* I was so embarrassed and ashamed that I never confided in her again. Plus the conversation created fear about looking bad at my job. So in the future, instead of staying home to take care of myself, I would load up on pain pills, drain all my energy, and get to work. Those days were useless—I couldn't remember from one moment to the next what I was asked to do. But I thought it was okay, at least I didn't look bad (or so I thought) in the eyes of this other woman because I was at my desk.

Is it beginning to make sense how powerful the combination of stress and shame are, and how they can run our lives? When experiences hit your shame triggers, it can be tough to stay grounded and move past the experience.

When I first started learning to recognize shame, the sensation felt like a knot in my stomach. I got sweaty and nervous and definitely didn't want to talk about it. However, shame, isolation, and feeling *not good enough* also manifest physically. Identifying stressors, beliefs, cultural imprinting, and shame triggers in all areas of life has allowed me to understand my perspective and subconscious beliefs. And that is important information!

Now, if that same coworker situation played out today, I would have stood up for myself and said something more like, "Maybe for you having your period doesn't equate to a sick day. But for me, menstrual cramps make migraines look like a walk in the park." And then I would not have given it a second thought. Because it is really none of her business how I spent my sick days; they are mine.

Think about recognizing shame as a powerful, innovative tool, albeit an uncomfortable one. Recognizing shame allows you to discover stuckness, stress, and negativity. Then you can use it to get one step closer to moving past the issue and onto personal growth. Recognizing shame will help you let go of unwanted negative thoughts and beliefs so you can create a life and a future that is right for you.

When we recognize shame, we can then choose our actions instead of feeling blindsided or kicked in the face with shame and then reacting. In these tender moments, we need a go-to person who listens empathetically and asks questions to help us understand our thoughts and feelings. Questions like: "How did you feel in that moment?" or "Why do you think you are having trouble letting go?" These questions are more helpful than a response like: "What a jerk! I wouldn't talk to that person ever again. Man, that happened to me once . . ."—and then the other person starts talking about herself and perpetuating the drama.

Sharing shame and vulnerability are an opportunity to witness our own courage and connect with someone who has earned the right to hear our stories. Connection helps us begin to feel like we belong, like we are worthy of love and acceptance. Then our relationship with the other person has an opportunity to become stronger, thus increasing self-confidence and self-worth.

Believe me, I know sharing is scary. Being vulnerable and revealing our true selves is a stripped-down-naked feeling. At first, I always wondered, *What if the other person doesn't get me? If they don't understand me, does that mean I am crazy?* I've had a variety of experiences, both when sharing goes well and when expressing myself didn't quite go as planned. The bottom line is about being authentic. So whether sharing goes as planned or not, it doesn't matter. Authentic sharing increases your experience of others accepting you for who you are, and in turn, your self-confidence grows.

Shame lives in how we think others perceive us. So separating our value from what others think squashes shame and stops the destructive effects it has on us. Practicing authenticity helps me become more myself, and letting go of what other people think gets easier.

One day not too long after I had been implementing this work, I found myself crying in the shower for almost an hour feeling guilty for not standing up for my health and myself sooner. I was ashamed of losing my voice and ashamed that it took me almost two decades to realize it. Finally, I dragged my shriveled self out of the shower and went straight to bed. I fell asleep in my robe for three hours. My husband got home from work to find me in bed, still in a robe, and my hair wrapped in a towel. In that moment, I had a choice. I could tell him about my afternoon or just give it a blanket description: "I'm not feeling well."

I was terrified to admit what I experienced; it was embarrassing. Remember how I didn't want anyone thinking I am weak or broken? In the split second prior to choosing, Brown's words were swirling around in my head: "Shame is healed between people . . . Sharing your experiences can deepen connections and build resilience . . . Shame thrives in silence; it wants you to keep the embarrassing experience to yourself . . . Shame loves isolation . . ." So I thought, *Here is my chance to practice the lessons I've been learning.*

I teared up and told Aaron how I was overwhelmed with guilt, how I spent an hour crying, and how the rush of emotions exhausted me for the rest of the afternoon. I was ashamed that I wasted half my life pretending to be fine and ashamed I wasted most of this day crying about it. I sat, sheepishly, awaiting his reaction to my embarrassingly pointless day. He told me he was proud of me and impressed with the huge progress I'd made with my health and healing in the last few years. He was glad I was able to let it all go and move on.

I exhaled. That wasn't so bad—and it only took a minute. Aaron understood me on a deeper level, plus I felt more confident for the next time shame came up. I could be honest with myself and authentically share. And it's true, as time went on, shame recognition and recovery has become much more speedy.

chapter 13

unconditionally me

*No matter what the problem is, our experiences are
just outer effects of inner thoughts.*
—Louise Hay, You Can Heal Your Life

Growing up, did you look up to a Southern Belle who would never consider cleaning her own home? Or did you grow up in the Midwest where you would never pay for something you could do yourself? Did your grandmother go to college? Does your aunt have no children and travel the world, or does she homeschool eight kids? Did your mother work 8:00 to 5:00, cook dinner, clean the house, *and* get kids off to their activities?

No matter what the answers are for you, they have shaped your thoughts and opinions about being a woman and a mother. We judge ourselves based on these learned cultural expectations and live accordingly. But what if you didn't have to live by the rules created by those around you? What if the reason you feel stuck in one area or another is because of these beliefs? What expectations would you let go of? What would you change about your life?

I resented cultural expectations about being a female. This manifested as rejection of any female household roles and any outward reflection of being a woman. As I look back, the pattern to refuse to adhere to the given gender rules showed up quite often in my life. Bitterness probably started as a young child when my mom told me I couldn't play outside without my shirt. It's not appropriate for little girls to not wear a shirt. *Lame!* My role rejection continued as my mom tried to make me wear a dress and to teach me to sew and to bake. Who wanted to do that? Not me.

As I got older, I realized that, at family gatherings, the women remained in the kitchen fixing dinner while all the men stayed in the living room watching football. I want to watch the game. Why couldn't I watch the game?

This mentality continued after college when I was living all alone in the big city of Houston and loving it! One day, the button fell off my favorite pair of black pants. I shipped them to my mom for repair. She didn't particularly appreciate the gesture. So for Christmas, she re-gifted the sewing box she gave me as a kid. She thought if I had all the tools to sew my own button, I might actually do it. But I didn't, much to my mom's dismay, "Didn't I teach you anything?" she concluded, "She just doesn't *want* to learn." It's true, I didn't want to learn to sew. I also didn't want to learn to ride a unicycle, but no one seemed to care about that. Now I take sewing jobs to the dry cleaner or a seamstress. And that sewing kit is back in the closet of my childhood room.

After I got married, feelings of failing as a woman and a wife bubbled to the surface. One of the most shameful things to admit to my family was the addition of our housekeeper. I could feel the disappointment in my mother's voice. "Audrey Michel, you can't even clean your own home?!" Apparently, it made me less of a woman. As guilt and shame built in the back of my mind, my Midwest values were telling me I was a bad wife. Good wives take care of their husbands by cooking, cleaning, and doing the laundry. I was taught if you can do it yourself, it is wasteful to pay someone else to do it.

My attempts to fit in were only holding me back. In order to let go of feelings of failure, I needed to find new examples of what being a modern woman could look like. Researching gender roles from other cultures helped me see that, even if I prefer to run our household differently than how I was taught, I'm not a bad wife. I finally let myself admit I wasn't going to be the wife I was raised to be.

I hated house cleaning. My husband hated it. And we constantly fought about who dusted the shelves or cleaned the toilet last. Seriously, the housekeeper has been one of the best decisions for our marriage.

Remember the topic about stress management? Well, while off-loading household chores helped, it is important to understand why hiring a housekeeper was the answer. If simply removing activities from my day-to-day schedule was the answer to less stress, why wasn't writing fewer blog posts the answer? Knowing what fulfills me and what drains me is key. Understanding where I am stuck because I'm not being true to myself allows me to identify what parts of my life can remain and expand and what parts need to be eliminated.

I'm going against the grain of my upbringing, and I am okay with that. Releasing guilt and resentment around not being the "right" woman relieved a lot of self-inflicted stress and shame. Letting go of others' expectations allowed me to get unstuck and move closer to being authentically me. It was a good feeling to get rid of things in my life that don't make me happy. Plus, letting go made more space for things that bring me happiness—best decision ever.

Part of accepting who I am as a woman was learning to love who I am as a woman. One liberating realization to come out of alternative healing was my struggle with unconditional self-love. Although I would never have previously described myself as struggling with loving the person I am, chronic pain was a giant roadblock in front of my self-love journey. When intense pain kept me in bed for days, self-love is the last thing I felt. My struggle with chronic pain and endometriosis lasted seventeen years; it had been around so long it had taken on a life of its own. Seventeen years is almost another adult person! I should have named it.

My thoughts never sounded like *I am unlovable.* I never looked in the mirror and thought *I'm ugly.* My negative thoughts were wrapped in sarcasm and sounded like, *I'm trading in my body. It's broken, and I want a new one.* Feeling beautiful on the inside didn't make sense to me. Anger and resentment do not coincide with light, airy, cheerful, joyous beauty. Intellectually, I could grasp what I've been through, but welcoming parts of myself that I previously pushed away took time. Welcoming self-love took practice and patience.

The Universe isn't short on hinting where we could use more unconditional love. When these hints go unnoticed, they become strong suggestions. Suggestions become swift kicks in the butt, and ass-kickings become full-on roadblocks. The Universe finally laid things out pretty clearly, saying, "I've been giving you choices and space to discover unconditional love for yourself for years, but now your only choice is to face your gremlins." I would like to say I wisely accepted the parts of myself and my life that I found undesirable and shameful all on my own, but I didn't. The truth is I hit rock bottom and had no other choice but to finally love myself for everything I am, everything I am not, everything I never wanted, and everything I hated. Finding self-love is like foolishly running away from home as an early teenager only to discover that finding food and shelter isn't that easy. As enthusiasm dissipates and hard realities sink in, turning around for home appears to be the only option. Facing my gremlins and finding unconditional love came with that same heavy, unbearable feeling of having to turn around and face home. It is awful, frightening, liberating, joyful, humbling, and everything in between.

———•———

As I embraced being a woman and began to love myself, it seemed one important question remained unanswered: To have kids or not to have kids? During kinesiology sessions, we worked on my ability to handle questions about motherhood, but we had not tackled the actual subject of being a mother. As healing progressed, I began to inch toward the conclusion that maybe having children isn't a part of my story.

The topic came to the forefront as my sister was pregnant and giving birth to my nephew. I remember chatting with her about the experience in the weeks following labor. Although her pregnancy experience was pretty smooth and uneventful, giving birth was not. As she shared her experience with me, I'm sure the expressions on my face were less than comforting. My body felt bloated with fear, and I squirmed with tension.

At that point in time, I could barely walk into OB-GYN offices without an anxiety attack, let alone tolerate an annual exam without falling into complete hysterics. The idea of pregnancy was physically and psychologically overwhelming for me, and my sister knew it. She commented that maybe having a baby isn't the best idea for me. I admitted that the idea of a fetus growing inside of me felt like having an amoebic parasite wreak havoc on my body, rather than a beautiful miracle. The process of renting my uterus out to another human being gave me the shakes. *Maybe she's right,* I thought. *Maybe pregnancy isn't the best decision for me.*

I sat with this idea for quite some time. What kept coming up for me was a curiosity about whether the decision was based on fear. And I knew it was. How would my body react? How would I emotionally react? *I can't even handle an annual exam once a year! OMG, a little person growing in my uterus and then getting pushed out of my vagina?* In seconds, the mere thought of having a baby had me trembling with fear. Too much trauma had already taken place in my reproductive organs. *Stretching and expanding to support another human? And then somehow my body expands for a six- to eight-pound person to find its way into the world? Seriously, not for me.* I couldn't get past it. My kinesiologist and I went to work addressing these fears and beliefs around pregnancy and motherhood.

Once I realized how afraid I was to be pregnant and to have

children, I needed to dig through the layers of why I was so scared. We made an interesting discovery.

I am the second of three children. Although, unless you really know my family, you would think I am the oldest. I actually have an older brother who passed away at twenty-seven hours old, after complications at birth. I cannot imagine the pain and grief my parents endured. Two years later, they were pregnant with me. The new pregnancy came with great joy and a new set of fears and anxiety for my parents. Through kinesiology, I discovered that while in the womb I took on a lot of the fear and anxiety my mother carried about losing another child. I then held those fears well into adulthood. These fears created subconscious beliefs that it is not safe to give birth, nor is it safe to care for an infant. This fear, along with dislike of my reproductive organs and resentment for being a woman, manifested as intense anxiety around the idea of having a family.

At thirty years old, I discovered, in addition to fear of pain, I was also running from someone else's fears and allowing those fears to define my life and my decisions. Now, let me be clear. I did not say my mom gave me her fears. I said my subconscious took them on. This was a powerful distinction for me. She did not give them to me, and it was hereditary; I am not a victim. I chose them, and I could choose to be done with them. This was an important shift. Putting it this way helped me think, *Huh, I don't need that anymore,* just as though I were cleaning out a closet.

Knowing what was going on for me brought me peace. I could embrace that my parents made it through their tough situation. I had taken on my mom's fears because I wanted her to feel comforted, which was a great thing to do, but now I know my mom is just fine. She survived the trauma and heartbreak and now has two grown married children and grandchildren. I've completed my job to help my mom get through her grief the best I knew how. But it no longer serves me, and it was time to move on.

The more fear we uncovered, the more connections I made

about my own behavior. From there, I could approach the topic of motherhood from inner wisdom, free of imprinting and unwanted influence. Now that it was emotionally safe for me to consider pregnancy, I was able to revisit the decision not to have children. This time I confidently accessed my heart center. What an unbelievably freeing feeling to know such a big life decision came from my heart and was wrapped in unconditional self-love!

Stripping away fear, I never felt more connected to my true self than I did once I finally admitted I didn't want to have babies. Aaron and I ultimately chose not to have children, and I am confident that the decision has come from a place free of fear and anxiety. The process of facing my fear of pregnancy helped me realize I never wanted to have children in the first place. What was missing for so many years was having a safe place within myself to explore my true feelings.

March 2012 is my line in the sand. The choice brought me internal healing, and my body relaxed like the weight of the world had been lifted. I felt lighter and more myself than ever. Now when someone asks when we are having children, I can easily and effortlessly respond, "We are not."

chapter 14

medical sexual trauma

When an eggshell cracks from the outside, it's crushed.
When it cracks from the inside, a being is born.
–Gabrielle Bernstein via Amma the hugging saint

By 2010, I had begun to address some of the major emotional trauma associated with the treatment of endometriosis. I made some major steps between 2008–2009, including the switch to holistic healing and quitting all pain medicine and most hormones. I was, however, still using birth control to regulate the timing and heaviness of my periods. In order to get yearly birth control refills, doctors required a checkup and a Pap smear. Annual exams became my yearly litmus test for where I was with physical and emotional healing.

Back in 2008, as I desperately sought out a new OB-GYN, one office bumped me to the top of their waiting list and agreed to see me immediately. Mary Lou, a nurse practitioner there, did what she could but ultimately passed me along to an endometriosis specialist. The specialist, although a great doctor, was a fertility specialist who focused on helping women with endometriosis get pregnant. As time went on, it became clear that I did not align with the realm of his practice. He wasn't particularly interested in seeing me for general gynecological needs, as I had no plans to use his fertility expertise. So I knew right where to go. Back to Mary Lou.

In 2010, as I drove to my yearly appointment, I was feeling confident since I had the symptoms under control. I sat in the waiting room of Mary Lou's boutique women's clinic, calm and collected, mindlessly reading a magazine on a beautiful, comfortable sofa. Mary Lou called me back and handed me a tiny plastic cup for a urine sample. I began to shake as I entered the spa-like restroom. The door closed behind me, and I didn't take another step. The shakes increased, taking over my body, and I cried giant, fearful tears. Although silent on the outside, I was screaming on the inside. Time stopped as the silly cup collected only my tears.

I was in there long enough for Mary Lou to quietly knock on the door. With her sweet voice, she asked, "Are you okay?" and interrupted the panic attack controlling my body. I opened the door, looked at her with my makeup-smeared eyes, and said nothing. I was paralyzed. I felt like every nerve ending was on fire. It was like I was in another galaxy while some unknown force controlled my body.

I was having a visceral reaction to the fear buried deep in my cells of what was about to happen in this office. So my body went into survival mode. This gazelle was about to be eaten by a cheetah.

She took the cup of tears from me, directed me to her office (not an exam room), sat me down, and handed me a box of Kleenex. I suppose she asked me questions. But all I remember is the inability to string together intelligible words, her hugging me and giving me a prescription for the upcoming year's birth control. Then I left. I sat in the car for an eternity, laying my head on the steering wheel and crying. When I was done crying, I tilted the seat back and just granted my body time to rest and recover before driving home.

When I got home, I called my kinesiologist for an emergency session. "All that visibly happened was I sat in a beautiful office, read a magazine, walked into a bathroom with a cup, a lovely woman hugged me, and handed me a piece of paper. And I am an emotional disaster," I told Deb. For the first time, I intellectually knew that fear and anxiety took over my body, and I experienced a panic attack.

It was confusing to witness myself go through this and know I couldn't emotionally separate past trauma from new experiences. My body hurt as if the annual exam physically happened. This marked the beginning of ever-so-delicately dealing with issues that I now know are medical sexual trauma.

I could clearly comprehend the fact that I had experienced various physical traumas throughout my life because of the treatment of endometriosis and living with chronic pain. I never thought much about any of it past *Yeah, that sucks*. As treatments turned holistic and began to focus inward, questions about sexual trauma seemed to pop up in kinesiology sessions. I didn't know it, but my reactionary patterns aligned with that of a sexual trauma patient. I always rejected the suggestion as I was never raped and no one ever purposefully hurt me in that way. But then I was presented with the term "medical sexual trauma," and everything fell into place. *Yup, I have that*. According to sex therapist Denise Onofrey, the person defines medical sexual trauma. It could be a birth, surgery, side effects of a medication, any procedure, condition, or incident that results in a trauma response. To acknowledge such a thing was huge—and the first step to healing it.

At the following year's exam, we skipped the urine test. Mary Lou simply checked my vital signs to ease into the appointment. Feeling confident again, as I had done so much work around the trauma still residing in my body and psyche, I proudly held it together until the cold, metal stethoscope touched my skin. I cried. But not hysterically this time, just soft silent tears. I guess I don't like metal medical instruments. I was elated that, although tears continued to roll down my face, Mary Lou and I were able to hold a coherent conversation. I agreed to a baby-step forward by choosing to talk in the exam room, but only if we sat in the side chairs and only after she put away the stirrups. I definitely wasn't ready to sit on the exam table. My tears continued throughout our discussion and the appointment.

She wrote out my prescription for birth control and inquired about how I was addressing the trauma. "Acupuncture, massage, and kinesiology are now a part of my life," I answered. "I've learned to recognize shame and trauma and not make myself wrong or feel bad for the amount of fear and anxiety trapped inside of me."

As we talked, she told me she wasn't interested in adding to the trauma and anxiety related to doctors and exams. As long as I was making progress in dealing with the trauma, she was willing to support me in whatever way I needed. She would move at my pace and support me in learning how to be fully in control. I was grateful that Mary Lou never asked me what happened. We both knew the damage was done, and there was no reason to revisit painful experiences. She was more interested in providing a space for me to feel safe. She continually checked in with me, and when I started to feel pushed outside my comfort zone to where we were doing more harm than good, we'd end the appointment.

For this particular annual appointment, being in the exam room was enough. Satisfied with our conversation, she gave me a hug, and I thanked her for allowing me to take baby steps. Mary Lou was patient with me about not having a Pap smear but continued to remind me that cervical cancer numbers increase after thirty, which I had already passed. She was comfortable with a break while I healed but wanted me to know that the break would come to an end. Yes, I knew.

Over the next year, my mind-body connection deepened, and so did my belief that the body is the message board to my psyche. I was paying attention to my body and the messages it sent me. It was that time of year again, and the weight of a Pap smear test was upon me. In the days following the phone call to make the appointment, stress, anxiety, and fear built up inside me. I actually gave myself hives, diarrhea, and cold sweats. According to Louise Hay's list in *Heal Your Body A-Z*, hives can be interpreted as small hidden fears and making a mountain out of a molehill. Diarrhea is fear, rejection, and running off. Cold sweats or chills are a mental contraction, a desire to retreat or respond with "leave me alone." All of these interpretations certainly applied to this situation.

As I walked into Mary Lou's office, I knew I was scared, but this time fear and anxiety didn't have a chance to take hold. My kinesiologist and I had worked to reinforce the fact that I was in control, to recognize my needs in the moment, and to have the courage to communicate them.

For the first time in five years, I made it through an entire exam. For the first time, I was in control and I asked for what I needed. Mary Lou supported me by doing whatever it took to make me comfortable.

Here is what I learned: I hate inanimate and unnatural objects touching me, especially metal. I chose to skip the blood pressure and vital sign check. It's always been in a good range, and it got in the way of our greater goal. Choosing for no stethoscope to touch me felt good; I was honoring my body. As I crossed the threshold of the exam room, the sight of exam table stirrups stopped me in my tracks. The awful stirrups were immediately put away; I couldn't even look at them. Next, we removed the crunchy, scratchy tissue paper from the exam table. I hated the noise it made and how it felt on my skin. I promptly decided I didn't want a paper gown either. The sound and feel of the stiff tissue paper irritated me to the core; it had to go. Mary Lou grabbed cotton gowns and asked if they would work. I held them and considered how my body felt. I felt calm. Cotton gown it is! We covered the exam table with a few more gowns in place of the tissue paper.

I was still nervous. Mary Lou returned to the exam room and asked where I would like to begin. Breast exam. Easy. Checking ovaries was equally easy, which surprised me. I guess I was fine with human touch. What terrified me were the medical instruments, and the cold metal touching my skin. Thank you, person who designed the speculum and brush used to gather cervical cells. Between that and transvaginal ultrasounds, it's no wonder my teenage self walked away with sexual trauma issues. Although Mary Lou used the smallest tools available, they were still metal, and I wasn't happy about it. I'll be honest, the test sucked. I was uncomfortable, and

I cried as the metal touched me. It makes me cringe to even write about it. The whole time Mary Lou reassured me that if I say stop, the exam will stop. But I didn't. I made it through and then cried tears of joy.

I didn't completely conquer medical sexual trauma that day. It still affects me. But I did cross the Golden Gate Bridge of fears to know I am no longer a prisoner of anxiety. I made it through the appointment without adding more trauma. And for that, I was proud.

I left with a strange mixture of feelings. Relieved. Exhausted. Scared. Confused. Proud. Starting New.

My biggest takeaway has been knowing that, within Mary Lou, I found another partner and teammate. She never once made me feel high-maintenance or like a pain in the ass. I never felt judged or embarrassed. She truly listened to me and did so at a time when my voice was small and quiet, scared and confused. I felt understood, and I felt worthy of asking for procedures to be done differently– to be done my way.

This safe environment in conjunction with kinesiology allowed me the safety of looking at the layers of the unrealized medical sexual trauma. Not only how trauma showed up in a doctor's office, but also how it showed up in other parts of life. Shame and trauma showed up several ways when it came to doctor's appointments. From painful procedures, to all male doctors, to believing my broken body could only be fixed by those in medical profession, it seems the treatment of endometriosis did as much damage as it did good.

The first layer I was able to acknowledge was that I believed medical appointments were not safe. No doctor was ever malicious in his intent. I was simply young and didn't understand what was happening. Exams were extremely painful, and I felt I didn't have a choice. I knew the doctors were trying to help me. I knew pelvic exams were part of the diagnosis, but they were so painful, and the pain would linger for days. I had repeatedly put the perceived importance of another pelvic exam above my own voice telling me it was unnecessary and that I didn't want to do it. I didn't feel safe; I felt hurt by someone I trusted. Each year, ever-increasing anxiety and conflict within my body sent me into a heightened state of stress and protectiveness. My subconscious swirled with negative thoughts: *Women around the world go through this without trouble...what is my problem? This shouldn't hurt; just get over it!* This much stress around one event was bound to get stuck in my body, mind, and spirit.

It never occurred to me that each exam was yet another traumatic event. It never occurred to me that I had a choice in whether pelvic exams were necessary. The most hurtful thoughts accumulated deep in my subconscious without my knowing: *My thoughts are not worth speaking; when it comes to my health, I do not know what I am talking about; I'm not worth the trouble.*

Years ago, I thought I was being strong and courageous in my ability to endure the exams. I know now that pushing through the pain and sucking it up was not the best way for me to deal with the situation. I held onto pain in my body tighter than a frightened kindergartener clinging to her mommy on the first day of school. It should come as no surprise, then, that I didn't have a favorable view of anyone who voluntarily tried to "fix" me. Only something broken needs to be fixed. For doctors, therapists, coaches, etc., it was a fine line between addressing the issue I came for and digging somewhere they didn't belong.

During the first twelve years of endometriosis treatments, I had all male doctors. It never occurred to me that I was giving my control to males who inherently had no idea what it felt like to deal with a painful, female reproductive disease. They had no way of understanding how I felt week to week, month to month, and year to year. And yet I believed they knew my body better than I did.

Interacting with males in positions of perceived power, like with doctors, turned out to be major contributors to shame. Experiencing shame is heightened when I don't feel heard or understood. Clearly the pattern of not feeling heard affected me at a doctor's office. I could comprehend that. Confronting shame triggers around any male in a perceived position of power was much more difficult. Only after I feel they understand me, and choose to meet where I am in the current moment, can we work together to move forward. However, if I sense at any time that a male is trying to fix, improve, or change me, I am instantly defensive. I revert to old, familiar tactics of hiding my true self and trying to look good, all while anger and resentment build inside.

Two stories exemplify the healing I had to find for expressing myself with males in perceived positions of power. In one situation, we successfully overcame my emotional trauma and continue to work together. In the other situation, I had to terminate our working relationship.

I want to start with Dr. Adam, my chiropractor.

My husband started seeing Dr. Adam in 2009. After experiencing great results, Aaron wanted me to go as well. "He is different," my husband explained, knowing that I didn't want to see a male doctor and feeling strongly that Dr. Adam's methods would be helpful for my ongoing back pain. Dr. Adam describes himself as a mixture between medical massage, trigger point release therapy, muscle rebuilding, and traditional chiropractic spinal manipulation.

It took Aaron about a year to convince me to visit Dr. Adam. At this point, I did know that male doctors were a source of emotional distress for me; however, I did not know the depth of distress. I was apprehensive but open to exploring what this guy had to offer.

As I walked into his office, my body was a jittery mix of cold sweats and shakes as I waited for Dr. Adam to join me in the exam room. My first impression: He is a very nice guy who genuinely wants to help people. He listened to my story, asked clarifying questions, and then proceeded to tell me his theory about pelvic pain and endometriosis. He believes the iliopsoas muscle is a contributing factor in a variety of ailments, including pelvic pain. Just so we are clear, the psoas (pronounced *SO-az*) is a muscle deep under the stomach and organs. It spans between the lumbar spine and head of the femur. The psoas runs the length of the torso. The ilium is basically the top and inside of your hip bone. The iliopsoas refers to a portion of the psoas muscle near the ilium. Think of pushing on the muscles in the space below the belly button and between hip bones. If you have endometriosis and/or pelvic pain, the thought probably makes you squirm—it does for me anyway! So our relationship was off to a rocky start.

Dr. Adam explained how he's treated several other women with endometriosis and chronic pelvic pain and had relieved back and abdominal pain by releasing the iliopsoas muscle, as well as hip and lower back muscles. But, to be honest, I didn't comprehend a word he said. He lost me at "belly button". My belly button is uber sensitive as it was the entry point for all four laparoscopy surgeries. Even the idea that it, or the area around my belly button, might be touched is a total deal breaker. I tried to explain this and where I was with the disease and different treatments. My voice quivered, and tears welled up in my eyes. As tears rolled down my face, I became more and more aware of how sensitive I was to male doctors. *How is this going to work?* I thought. *I should be honest with him, right? I should just tell him why I am so upset. . . but then it doesn't even make sense why I'm here.* Exhale.

"I hate male doctors," I suddenly blurted.

Dr. Adam looked at me.

"And I am extremely sensitive, so for this to work, we have to go at my speed. I don't care if I put your children through college. I am not in a hurry. I am an onion, my layers have to be peeled back. You can't just slice through me."

Exhale. There, I said it. My head hung down as I pretended my only soggy Kleenex was doing its job.

He smiled, took a deep breath, and told me it was okay. He

understood. *Wow,* I thought, *not the reaction I expected.* He then asked how I felt about laying on the chiropractic table, as he'd like to see how my muscles felt. Still a sobbing mess, but feeling a level of understanding, I hopped on the table. The only thing going through my head was how much I didn't want another guy touching me or trying to fix me. This should have been a red flag, but it was early in my journey of listening to my body, and I said nothing.

He gently poked around at my back and legs. Tears dripped down the side of my face and eventually onto the table. As he tried to learn more about my body and the state of my muscular system, all I could think was, *I hate being poked. It makes me feel like a lab rat.* I could feel myself becoming more and more irritated. And then he poked my stomach.

Oh, hell, no! I yanked his hand away from me and yelled about how my stomach is off limits. I covered my face as I bawled. I don't recall much as I lie there crying. I was upset and embarrassed. He said he was sorry and was going to leave the room, letting me know I could take as much time as I needed.

Lord knows how long it took me to collect myself. I did as well as I could, scurried through the waiting room full of people, paid my bill, and scheduled another appointment. Why would I schedule another appointment? Nodding yes to "Next week at this time?" seemed easier than explaining why I never wanted to come back. The room was spinning; I couldn't even focus. Physical pain took over. Apparently, I got in my car, drove a few blocks, pulled over, and called Aaron to come get me.

Pain, exhaustion, and shock kept me in bed for three days following my initial consultation with Dr. Adam. That first night I experienced radiating, stabbing pain from my abdomen and back. As I tossed and turned, trying to ignore the throbbing pain and to get comfortable, I yearned for the pain pills that used to sit on my bedside table. *I'll do anything for this awful feeling to go away,* I thought. I broke down, crying, desperate, and angry. I couldn't go back to that place of desperation, where taking pain pills seemed like a good decision.

I couldn't believe a man barely touching my stomach could take me to this angry, painful place. *I've worked too hard to get where I am, off pain pills and functioning in society, to go back to a life of pain. Why would I choose to do something that brought the pain back?* My thoughts were spinning. Just as my experiences with Mary Lou had shown me, I was beginning to understand the power my history had over my current experiences.

Once recovered, I decided returning to Dr. Adam's office wasn't the best for me. The thought made me sick to my stomach. I'd worked too hard to return to desperate, angry feelings and thoughts of taking pain pills. However, as time went on, I got curious about why I reacted so severely to Dr. Adam touching my stomach. It was not a harsh action by any means, just gently pushing to feel muscles and organs. Why would my body hurt so badly from this guy barely touching me? I can push on my stomach all day, and my body couldn't care less. Three days in bed with excruciating pain? It didn't make any sense to me, and I wanted to know more.

My kinesiologist and I began working to release the trauma and fear around working with male doctors. Deb and I worked on understanding the emotions held within my stomach and psoas muscles and subsequent reactions. I've always known my stomach and belly button were sensitive, but this experience was extreme. Working through medical sexual trauma took several years of ongoing and complicated baby steps. Just as my mind protected itself by pretending all the trauma didn't exist, my body made steel cables out of my muscles to protect itself. And just like mentally relaxing meant vulnerability to my emotions, physically relaxing meant trapped trauma might explode out of me.

Much of the work Deb and I did revolved around making it safe for me to express myself around males and safe for my body to release the tension it used as protection for so many years. The psoas muscle holds much emotion, especially for women with reproductive issues, and even more so for sexual trauma patients. So any bodywork to release psoas tension for me couldn't be done directly, at least not at first.

Breathing and staying grounded in the current moment have helped me understand that even though current experiences are reminiscent of the past or bring up painful memories, I am in a better place. I can deal with current experiences differently, communicate what my body needs, and be in control of my path to wellness.

Six months after walking out of Dr. Adam's office, a little voice in the back of my head started wondering how I might react differently after working through more layers of physical and emotional issues, and taking baby steps toward healing medical sexual trauma. I indeed returned, and neither Dr. Adam nor his staff ever discussed the disastrous day. I appreciated feeling welcomed into a judgment-free environment, and my body responded just as well.

We began by addressing outlying muscles, not my psoas! As muscles released, and scar tissue was eliminated, I needed simultaneous emotional work to deal with buried feelings stirred up by bodywork appointments. Addressing mental and emotional issues simultaneously allowed my body to accept and integrate treatment from Dr. Adam.

I continued to see Dr. Adam twice a month for a couple of years, and I thought my body was making great progress. One day, Dr. Adam walked into the exam room and went straight for my most sensitive back muscle. He barely touched me, but my body flipped out. Flashes of darkness and lightning bolts of pain raced through my body. I yelped and started bawling. I'm sure Dr. Adam knew I was crying, but since I was face down, I doubt he understood the explosion of emotion spilling out of me. Bless his heart, he was talking to me about the way our bodies carry emotion and how bodywork can release those feelings. I knew he was trying to make me feel better, but it didn't matter.

As the internal darkness faded, my head throbbed. Dr. Adam continued talking in an attempt to calm me down. However, it had the opposite effect. The more he spoke, the more irritated I got until I burst, "The sound of your voice makes me want to vomit! Please leave."

He quietly walked out and shut the door to the exam room. I lay there for a moment waiting for my head to stop spinning. *Really?* I thought to myself, completely deflated. *WTF was that?* I finally got up, found a tissue, cleaned the makeup mess from my face, and sat in the chair for a while. As I put on my shoes and coat, I thought, *Good grief. I still have to walk out of here and pay. Ugh! Where do I come up with this shit?* Embarrassed, I put on my sunglasses, dug my phone out of my purse, and hurried through the waiting room totally pretending to text. After paying, I asked his massage therapist if I could talk to her. We stepped out of the office. I broke down crying and asked her to apologize to Dr. Adam for my rude behavior. She hugged me and told me not to worry about it. They understand visceral reactions and emotions released by bodywork. "You're not the only one," she said. I exhaled again.

Dr. Adam and I joke about this story now. And I repeatedly thanked him for not only understanding and giving me space, but also for not making me feel like a lunatic. Hearing that I am not crazy felt good, and I have another teammate who meets me where I am on my wellness journey. I have been seeing him regularly ever since.

———

The second experience that brought medical sexual trauma to the surface was with a business coach. This was 2012, which marked the culmination of my healing and wellness journey. I was not only pain-free and symptom-free, I no longer relied on any medications to regulate my hormones, which was something I was very proud of and openly shared. I thought that because I had physically found wellness, I was, therefore, emotionally and spiritually healed.

The coaching situation was designed to find *your why* and build a business around it. This process meant more digging than I was prepared for. The idea sounded perfect; however, my historic pattern of separating my health problems from the rest of my life showed up again. It didn't take too many questions to uncover insecurities and internal unrest.

The business coach was in a perceived position of power—he had knowledge and experience that I wished to gain—giving us a slight disadvantage. So did the fact that, up until that point, endometriosis discussions happened only with women or a professional who sensed my unease with the topic and respected where I was. I told him how sensitive I was about talking about my health with males. But as time went on, he poked, prodded, and questioned every insecurity, fear, and gremlin living in my subconscious. Intellectually, I understood that his intended process was to dig deeply, hoping to discover the why of me and, therefore, uncover what would ultimately bring me happiness in business. But that's not how my story went.

Coaching went straight for my most painful weaknesses. Shame triggers fired as I struggled to sort out my thoughts. I felt exposed and embarrassed. I did my best to hide where my psyche was headed, to look good in front of this business professional, but the gremlins were getting the best of me. My need to feel heard and understood flared up quickly and often.

The medical sexual trauma inside of me went into overdrive: *You're not listening to me; you're hurting me; why would you do this to me?* raced through my brain. As our monthly meetings carried on, my anxiety surrounding potential health questions increased. I didn't want to talk about my health, but I felt I didn't have a choice. I thought if I didn't answer him, then I was choosing not to move my business forward. I hired him, so I needed to do what he said. The downward spiral of shame was in full effect, and my emotions were in control. My voice was powerless. Sounds like the underlying emotions of a doctor visit, huh?

At our final meeting, I began to grasp just how misunderstood I had been. Much of the conversation is a blur, but the gist of the issues arose from a comment about how I continually took three steps forward and two steps back. In my optimism, I answered that I felt one step forward was progress. He laughed at me. Built-up anger from our time working together boiled in my belly. Shame triggers activated every insecurity, and a year's worth of feeling like he was trying to fix me flashed through my body. My brain was scrambled. Internal darkness was closing in, and tunnel vision turned to dizziness. I remember sweating and feeling pains in my stomach as he said he was tired of the setbacks.

He began talking pointedly about where we stood. Any actual words disappeared, and his voice sounded like a twelve-year-old pounding on a drum set. My legs trembled with anger. I couldn't even look at him. I vividly remember the beautiful abstract paintings behind him– a needed distraction from the awful conversation. The more he talked, the more my brain swirled and fire rose up in my throat. I blurted out that I needed him to stop talking.

At this point, I recognized I was knee-deep in shame. I suggested I needed a break in the conversation. We sat in silence, and his eyes seemed to burn a hole through me. I finally found the courage to quietly tell him I could no longer participate in any previous commitments, and we awkwardly parted ways.

The experience brought me to finally accept that the medical sexual trauma affected interactions with the opposite sex, not just doctors. When I continually feel unheard, I head down the path of a psychological rape case. When *no* doesn't mean *no*, I feel threatened and harmed. I lose my voice, my power, and my grounding.

I chose to write an email about how things played out for me. Although the email was to him, it was really for me. I needed to be extremely honest and authentically me, all the imperfect ugliness of me. The email represented fifteen months of bottled up anxiety, pretending I was fine, trying to look good, and losing. It represented the culmination of almost two decades of disease and loss of power. I put others' opinions ahead of my own. I valued others' judgments over my own authenticity. I struggled to accept myself and my story. That is, until I hit send.

For the first time, I was completely free of the outcome and detached from another's opinion of me. For the first time, I understood that being authentic connected me to who I am and gave me confidence to be vulnerable. I knew that regardless of the outcome, I could stand on my own two feet. And I did.

I am not suggesting that the answer to authenticity is to go around telling off the world, spewing anger at anyone in your path. I am, however, suggesting that if you are going to share deep, hurtful parts of yourself, having a professional team to assist you in letting go of negative thoughts, beliefs, and shame is key. Surround yourself with people who support you the way you need to be supported and let go of those who do not.

—•—

One night at a thirty-fifth birthday dinner with a group of friends, someone asked the birthday girl if she had had a midlife crisis yet, to which she answered, "no." Someone else commented that she hadn't either and hoped she never does.

I sat in silence, contemplating my last few years as I've physically, emotionally, mentally, and spiritually overcome endometriosis and chronic pain. A warm sense of gratitude came over me. My mask is off. I am grateful for the wisdom of intuition and insight to listen to my body and my heart. It's when we get so off track and drift so far away from our true selves and true paths that the "midlife" crisis hits. If I ever get that far off track again, hell yes to the midlife crisis.

So what have I learned from these years of overcoming pain and disease? The same situation often plays out over and over until we choose to learn the lesson. It will be disguised differently, but the lesson will be the same. We either learn it, or we don't. If we don't, it will show up again and again. If we do, we get to move on to the next lesson, allowing us to grow, and we continue to get closer to being the person we are meant to be.

The biggest lesson has been to be unapologetically, authentically me. Even in the most hurtful situations, being my true self makes for the most genuine relationships. Second, the ability to listen to my body and recognize when a relationship or situation isn't working is an essential part of healing. I know it is possible and essential to surround myself with people and practitioners who understand my situation and me. I will always fight for myself and for my health.

chapter 15

listen to your body

Trust the voice within.
–Echo Bodine

You know how people say to listen to your gut? Listening to your body is like that but more intricate and ongoing. We tend to reserve "listen to your gut" for big decisions, but listening to your body is for every moment. I am constantly noticing and analyzing how I feel in one situation or another as every sensation and feeling means something. I check in with myself and ask, "How am I feeling right now?" If I feel good, what am I thinking about, who am I with, what have I eaten, or have I exercised? And the same questions apply if I don't feel so good.

Every moment is an opportunity for feedback and learning. Every moment is an opportunity to be curious and to grow. Our bodies create sensations to communicate when there is emotional, mental, and spiritual pain. Long ignored communications in the emotional body can manifest as pain and/or disease. My body had been screaming at me for years to examine thoughts and beliefs around being a woman, being a mother, and around medical sexual trauma. I ignored my body for far too long.

Years ago, as I sat crying over a pile of pills, I didn't cheer with joy celebrating that my body was communicating with me. I was having a complete breakdown. Underneath it all, I was about to make one of the best decisions of my life. I knew something wasn't right and finally surrendered. I was scared, but I knew I was supposed to learn something. That day marked a turning point for me to trust the feedback my body is giving me. It sparked a journey of curiosity and a process to untangle the balled up mess of wires attempting to function as my emotional body and internal wisdom.

As I progressed through bodywork therapies, it became more and more obvious to me just how much information our bodies hold. Every cell in my body holds emotion and memory of past experiences. This can be both helpful and hurtful. As I now know, I don't want to hold negative issues in my tissues! And I didn't want to ignore signs pointing me toward becoming authentically me. I know my body and myself well enough to distinguish between the two. So how did I get to this point?

For physically manifesting ailments, I use *Heal Your Body* to help me figure out what area of life I need to look at. For example, during my most recent visit to Mary Lou, as I was sitting on the exam table sporting the latest trend in hospital gowns, my eyes began to itch. They were increasingly itching so badly that I couldn't stop rubbing my eyes.

All of a sudden I caught myself, stopped, and looked at Aaron. "Look at Louise Hay's list. What does it say for eyes?"

"The capacity to see clearly and not liking what you see in your life."

"Ok, now what about itching?"

"Itching, to get out or get away."

I smiled and laughed to myself. I closed my eyes, got quiet, and mentally repeated that I am at peace and I am safe. I am confident Mary Lou will support whatever I need for this appointment to be a success. It didn't take long for the itching to subside and my eyes to return to normal.

There is absolute power in listening to your body and making sense of any breakdown, big or small. Recognizing that every issue carries physical, emotional, and spiritual weight opened me up to incredible healing. A headache is no longer just a headache. It's self-doubt or self-criticism, and as soon as I know where it is coming from, I can let it go.

Combining Louise Hay's knowledge of mental thought patterns manifesting physically with Brené Brown's work on authenticity and shame created an effective self-discovery power-punch. I love the way Brown puts it, "A breakdown is an opportunity for a breakthrough." Shifting my thinking from fearing breakdowns to welcoming growth opportunities gave new meaning to everyday experiences.

Pay attention to how your body feels in every moment, especially emotionally hurtful situations. Does your body feel light and airy, or heavy? Pay attention to what events get stuck in your mind. Do you wish you handled something better? Do you wish you could go back and express yourself differently? Are you replaying the highlight reel in your mind? This is a key indicator. Ask yourself what are you struggling to let go of. What do you need to identify and acknowledge for yourself? What is the gift within the situation?

Asking questions and being open to new possibilities and new perspectives is great, but until you are able to listen to your body and integrate what is right for you, none of this will work. How many times have you read *The Fastest Way for a Better [insert whatever]* and it made no difference? Made a New Year's resolution that was going to change your life that you forgot by the Super Bowl? Or your best friend said she has the best massage therapist, and because of her she no longer gets headaches, so you took her business card but have yet to make a phone call.

Currently, in my mid-section on the left side, my body feels stuck. I call it Sticky Rib. I have a chiropractor whom, as I've mentioned, I now adore. For the longest time, I was frustrated because we couldn't get Sticky Rib to go away. You know when you twist one way and a stuck rib gabs you in the lungs (or so it feels)? That rib of mine has a lot to say. On the surface, it appears to obviously be a muscular-skeletal issue easily fixed by putting it back into place and balancing the surrounding muscles. We did this for months with little success. For months we blamed it on poor posture, being an obsessed author chained to my desk, or my dwindling yoga practice. And yes, these things contributed to the issue, but guess what—the root cause of Sticky Rib isn't a muscular problem. It took me a while to realize the issue wasn't a physical issue. Sticky Rib is where I store unwanted stress, especially medical sexual trauma and feelings of not being enough. Once I acknowledged the issue lived in my emotional body, I was able to make progress toward letting issues go and decreasing my body tension.

During a kinesiology session with Deb, we did visualization therapy around medical sexual trauma. I had a vivid image of the trauma showing up like a third arm connecting to my body at Sticky Rib location. Within the visualization, Deb asked why it was so painful. I answered that I had been chopping off this arm with a hacksaw repeatedly for years trying to get rid of it, yet each time it grew back angrier than before. Deb asked, "If chopping it off isn't working, why do you continue to do it?" I cried as I realized I wasn't using the tools I've learned. Chopping off a part of myself is not unconditional love. Deb asked if I could welcome the third arm of Sticky Rib back into my body, integrate it into my being, and love it just as much as I love any other part of myself. Yes, I could.

Over the next week, as my body integrated the emotional changes we made, Sticky Rib physically relaxed. I now go long stretches without hearing from Sticky Rib, but it still speaks up every now and then. Unresolved medical sexual trauma activated Sticky Rib, and so does any unloved part of me. The discomfort of Sticky Rib comes and goes much quicker now that I understand its origin. I welcome aggravation as an indicator and locator for potential growth.

Being aware that your body is taking on stress of any kind is a big step forward in listening to your body. Step two is to distinguish whether the stresses are your own or if you are taking on someone else's. A big take-away from kinesiology has been the ability to differentiate between my own stresses and those of other people. Not only is my body sensitive, but I'm also empathetic, which means I like to take on other people's stress. Not the most helpful habit.

Have you ever gone to lunch with someone and all she did was talk about herself? Complaining about this problem or that problem then telling you her opinion about how awful this person or that person is. By the time lunch is over, you've noticed you aren't sitting very tall. You aren't feeling all that upbeat. Maybe you have a headache. You realize this other person just vomited her yuckiness all over you. This is what I'm talking about.

Once I went to a convention to see Dr. Wayne Dyer speak. I assumed the crowd would be full of people just like me, those interested in self-help and inspiration and maybe some coaches and spiritual leaders. What I didn't see coming was the number of sick people seeking healing, which I totally understand since he is a powerful man. I, however, never thought about activating a protective bubble around myself to protect against taking on stress, feeling upset, and pain from other people. So I walked out of there bloated with stress and negativity. Thank goodness, I could recognize the stress as not mine and let it go.

Ask yourself, "Is this mine or that of the environment?" If it's the environment's, shake it off and let it dissolve into the Universe. If it is your own stress, fill your toolbox with ways to repair your own issues. I use a couple of techniques to listen to my body. I begin with a method of checking in with my body, or body checking. I sit quietly, close my eyes, let my awareness shift inward, and listen. I slowly scan my body from head to toe. I am looking for anything that feels off. Is there any pain, stiffness, tension, discomfort, throbbing, etc.? If the scan only makes it to my shoulders, that is fine. That is where the issue is located for this moment. I sit with the discomfort, not making it good or bad, not forcefully thinking about how it needs to go away, just noticing. Sometimes it is as simple as telling the bit of discomfort, "Hey, I notice you." And that is enough for it to dissipate.

Body checking is a way to give space to my truth in a supportive, nonjudgmental way that allows it to safely come out of hiding. If what comes up is a negative thought, it usually just needs a light on it for me to let it go. Again, I am just noticing and acknowledging what is coming up, and usually that is enough to let the issue go. I don't get upset with myself or try to force positive thoughts into the space.

When the issue is heftier, I ask myself, "What's the scary thing I don't want to look at?" I use a technique I like to call energy movement. I place my hand over the area that feels stuck and return to the place of inner relaxation and reflection. I put my attention on the area under my hand and sit with the discomfort. Again, I ask myself questions like, "What is it I need to know?" I do my best to radiate unconditional love through my hands to the cells in my body that need attention. I give my body the same love and understanding I would give to a toddler that bumped his head. I sit with the pain or discomfort and radiate love.

As I work through energy movement, sometimes my body throbs or feels hot. Sometimes I feel bloated with energy or have tight muscles. Sometimes I feel more relaxed, and other times I may not. Sometimes I feel energy escaping through my fingertips, and I flick it off me. Other times energy escapes through my toes, and I just let negative energy drain out of me. When my body feels complete, I awaken my body and mind by wiggling my fingers and toes and introducing movement back into my limbs and core. Then I slowly open my eyes. Afterward, I tend to feel more balanced and lighter.

Other times, discomfort needs more attention. Listening to my body sometimes means a change in perspective. For example, as I worked through medical sexual trauma issues and listened to Sticky Rib, I realized I needed a different perspective. For as long as I can remember, when I thought about pelvic exams or internal ultrasounds, my view was of me lying on an exam table fearing pain. One day, I wondered what it was like for the doctors and nurses involved. How did my doctor feel about examining a fourteen-year-old? All of a sudden I felt the compassion and urgency they had to help me feel better. I imagined my doctor radiating love for a person in pain. For the first time, I could see the situation from a positive angle. This new perspective opened the floodgates of healing medical sexual trauma.

———

Unlike body checking and energy movement, which I use for situational issues, meditation is a daily practice meant to bring a person to a place of balance, connect him or her to themselves, and move forward in personal growth. Many types of meditation have varying intensity and skill levels. My meditation journey began with sitting quietly and asking my body what I need to know today. That technique brought benefits for a while, but I felt uneducated about what I was doing– like I was making it up. So I shifted to the Deepak Chopra and Oprah meditation challenges. I enjoyed guided meditation and topics to meditate on and journal around. But again, about three months into it, I felt that progress stopped.

I shared my struggles with my kinesiologist, and she was happy to hear I was headed in the direction of meditation. She suggested I look into Transcendental Meditation (TM). What I was most attracted to with this method was the involvement of a teacher, somebody to talk to.

Now, the way everyone talks about meditation, I thought it was supposed to be sunshine and happy faces. Help relieve stress and help me connect to my whole self. Doesn't that sound beautiful? As an overall, yes, meditation is a valuable tool. However, in the beginning, it caused an absolute shitstorm of emotions for me. Meditating opened the floodgates for past stresses to poor out of my body, and the dam broke. All of the hurt, anger, pain, and ugliness from my life was given an instant escape. And it came out of my face. I broke out with painful, flaky, eczema-like acne like I'd never experienced. I felt jittery and angry, wanting to yell about everything. I didn't understand. *Haven't I already done the work to get rid of this crap? How is there more?* At first, I thought I just needed better meditation skills; I must be doing it wrong.

This is where having a teacher is key. I had someone to talk to, someone with experience to explain that meditation activated the release of decades' worth of unwanted ugliness. My teacher helped me through it and explained that even though I thought I needed more meditation to get rid of how awful I felt, I actually needed less to stop how overwhelming it was. I intellectually understood that meditating was getting rid of old stress and ugly feelings, and that in the long run I would benefit, but I hated it for the moment. We dialed down the duration and frequency of meditation, knowing that when my body was ready I would return to full sessions. Backing off TM is what I needed for my sensitive body. I returned to a small meditation practice and have been taking baby steps toward a full practice. I continue to listen to my body to see how much meditation I am ready for.

No matter what type of meditation you choose to practice, each practice, just like every day, is different. There are ups and downs, and that is okay. Meditation at its core is meant to release stress and repair glitches in the nervous system. Because of meditation I am calmer and less affected by chaos around me. It's as if I can see and understand any craziness surrounding me but now choose not to participate in a way that affects my body. I can watch the situation and interact if needed but no longer get caught up in stress, drama, chaos, or negativity. And if I feel myself getting pulled into any of it, I take a break and check in with my body.

I cannot reiterate enough the importance of continually

checking in and asking yourself, "Am I doing what is best for me and my health? Am I aligned with the energy of inner wisdom?" Sound like a big commitment and a lot of work? It is at first, but then it becomes a way of life. Listening to my body is a muscle I've had to strengthen over time.

Body checking, energy movement, and meditation are a huge part of self-care. Part of doing what's best for me is maintaining a routine of honoring my body so I can show up successfully for all parts of my life. I view anything that creates a positive energy shift as self-care. For me, getting up before 7:30 a.m. is not self-care. My body absolutely requires eight hours of sleep, and usually I get more. I like to eat breakfast around 9:30 a.m. My mornings are slow, and I've accepted that, even though the early bird gets the worm, this bird rises slowly. My work brain gets going around 10:00 a.m., and that is fine. Unconditionally loving myself means accepting that I could potentially cross more off my list if I would get my butt going earlier, but I know that my first self isn't my best self. It takes a bit of time and a self-care routine to get my best self going. Food choices used to be a much bigger part of my life than they are now. Dietary choices are so ingrained in me, I barely notice. Junk food, fast food, sugar, preservatives, and anything cold is the devil; I feel like crap instantly, and I know it. So I avoid all of it. My body needs movement. I do yoga– the easy, stretchy kind. I'm no longer an extreme athlete and have embraced my softer, more feminine body.

Honoring yourself and your body is about finding joy, fulfillment, and saying yes. Yes to a weekday matinee. Yes to a Bloody Mary on the golf course. Yes to a horseback ride or a weekend with new friends. Yes to an afternoon nap. I said yes to an impromptu flight home to watch football with my two-year-old nephew, and it was awesome. I said yes to a women's conference in New York City that has profoundly affected me. I said yes because I could feel the potential for joy warming my body, and in honoring this part of myself, I became more connected to myself.

Healing my body and mind has been a process of peeling back

layer after layer and continuing to learn about myself, greeting the new information with love and compassion. With each layer that physical and emotional turmoil presented, I trusted the process of releasing negative thoughts and feelings. Addressing physical and emotional issues complemented each other. As I grew emotionally, I became more aware of my body's physical needs and found value in honoring and healing my body.

chapter 16

heal vs. cure

You can cure without healing, and you can heal without curing.
—Dr. Lissa Rankin, Mind Over Medicine

The medical community defines cure as eliminating all evidence of disease and restoring the body back to where it was before illness, focusing on the physical body and relieving discomfort, pain, illness, and disease. I have to be honest, for most of my life this sounded exactly like what I wanted. Get rid of this endometriosis crap, and give me my body and life back. Yes, endometriosis is an incurable disease. Many physicians and surgeons believe that if they can rid the body of endometriosis tissue then patients will be pain and symptom-free, which is a great goal and a path worth pursuing. The idea and path of eliminating endometriosis tissue sufficed for many years. Until it didn't. In my case after my final surgery, I was free of endometriosis tissue, but not pain-free or symptom-free.

The Western medicine process is reductive, meaning physicians will filter down issues and symptoms to discover the base physiological cause of the problem. On one hand, you finally get to discover what the problem is and what to do about it. Find a solution and the problem is solved. When it comes to singular issues like a broken leg or a sinus infection, there is a clear solution, and the medical community excels at solving these problems. But with endometriosis and other complex diseases, it's not so cut and dry—every case is different. Did I need the medical community to identify the disease, locate the unwanted cells, and eliminate endometriosis tissue? Absolutely, without a doubt. But when it came to the many layers of pain and symptomatic issues, reducing my problems down to endometriosis and eliminating the existence of endometriosis cells would not eliminate my problem.

In not so many words, my physician and endometriosis specialist told me there was nothing more they could do for me. And it was true. They had used up all the tools in their toolbox. And that is okay. Think about it this way: An American hair dryer won't work in Europe. But it is not because the hair dryer is broken; it's because the electrical outlet and the power cord don't use the same voltage. So, there I was trying to shove my American hair dryer into a European outlet. I thought if I bought more American hair dryers and just bent the prongs this way or that way, pushed harder, or searched for a new outlet, sooner or later I'd be able to dry my soaking wet hair. But I needed a European hair dryer. Once I knew where to look, I discovered my "European hair dryer" of holistic healing.

Don't get me wrong. I believe we need a cure for endometriosis, just like we needed a cure for polio and we need a cure for cancer. We need a cure for many things, and I will continue to do my part to raise awareness and funds for research. However, what do those of us currently living with an incurable disease do? It is a slippery slope to put all our hopes for a better life in something or someone other than ourselves.

At the time, never did I imagine my body, mind, and spirit were telling me it was time for a new direction. The Universe had been hinting at it for years, and I couldn't hear it.

Once I began to gain knowledge about the possibilities of healing from within, acquiring tools to strengthen my mind-body connection became mission number one. Although Western medicine stopped the process of disease, it was not going to heal my whole body. That was up to me. On the fateful day I quit taking pills, I had a tiny thought that maybe my body hated the pills and was urging me to stop. I had an inkling that there could be more available than the medication that was getting me nowhere. So I listened to my body beyond conventional logic. Think about it, would I have actually quit the medication if I logically weighed all the options? What if I waited for the perfect day when my emotions weren't all over the place, pain was under control, and I was ready to intellectually consider my future? My logical brain would have told me pain was too much to handle. Logic would have told me what it always told me– I need the pain pills. But that day, sitting on the edge of my bed, I went with my gut. I listened as intuition pulled me in another direction.

My energy shifted, the medicated fog lifted, and I felt like myself. Sure, I was still in pain. I still had rough days. I was still exhausted. But for the first time in a long time, I felt like *myself.* The more I reconnected to myself, the more I wanted to get rid of anything that wasn't me. I surrendered and said, "Yes, I have endometriosis. Yes, I live with chronic pain. Yes, I've been hiding it. Yes, my life is a f-----g mess." Instead of wanting my life restored, I went about creating a new, better life.

Healing takes time, patience, and persistence—and a belief that your body can heal. Need proof? Our bodies do it every day. Have you ever cut your finger? Did you run to the doctor? Do you believe that a bandage would make it better? Or did you trust that your finger would heal in a few days?

Healing the whole body, mind, and spirit happens on a deeply personal level. It comes from within, from the core of our being. It is an uncomfortable, mentally and emotionally draining process to painstakingly identifying negative patterns, thoughts, and beliefs; let go; and develop new positive patterns free of shame. Every aspect of life has to be inspected and revamped.

Like everything else we've been discussing, healing starts with looking at what feels the easiest to tackle. How do you spend your time? Who do you surround yourself with? What are you doing to acknowledge and manage stress? When you feel pain, do you connect with inner wisdom? Do you ask your body what it's trying to say? Are you nourishing your mind and body with the things that bring you joy? Are you making choices that get you one step closer to being fulfilled? Are you honoring your body?

Years ago if you would have asked me if I was respecting my body, I would have said yes. Now I know better. Injecting chemicals, ingesting toxins, eating junk, overexercising, overworking, ignoring stress, ignoring my body, and not putting much thought into the people I chose to spend my time with was collecting and storing negativity in every cell of my body. Sure, I was taking care of myself in a traditional sense. I seemed healthy, right? But I put my needs for whole body wellness last.

Healing is re-inventing and re-creating ourselves, not fixing or restoring the old. Healing removes the obstacles that prevent the mind, body, and spirit from working together. Heal your soul first, and it will teach your mind and body what they need to do the same.

Am I cured of endometriosis? No, it is an incurable disease. I am, however, pain-free and symptom-free of endometriosis. I am healed from a painful disease that ruled my life for seventeen years. I have not returned to the life I knew before the disease. I have a new life– one that I was meant to live.

chapter 17

celebration, joy, gratitude

Love. Heal. Celebrate.
–Personal mantra

n March 2012, after being off all other pills for over three years, I chose (with much consideration from the health professionals around me) to quit taking birth control. I had been taking birth control since I was diagnosed at fourteen as a way to regulate my heavy, painful cycle. At thirty-one, once we decided not to have children, I no longer needed the hormones to prevent pregnancy, so why was I taking them? For years I was scared to trust that my body could regulate itself. But in the months prior to this decision, I had been beginning to sense that birth control was more of an emotional crutch than a necessity.

I wanted to know if my body could function without pills. This decision became a test to see if I was as well as I wanted to be. I had to try even though I was scared. I'd been on birth control for over half my life. Letting go of the belief that I needed it, that my body relied on it, that I couldn't function without it was a big hurdle. But I finally said, "I'm ready; I've had enough."

Now that my body was functioning well and healing was well underway, the decision to quit birth control had been a long time coming. It felt good to have the courage to make it. In the time since quitting hormones to regulate my cycle, I've felt free. My body did what it is supposed to do. In fact, my body functioned better than ever. My cycle is lighter and literally unnoticeable. (Now I'm the annoying girl who forgets she is getting her period and is totally unprepared. I used to hate that girl). I no longer have pain or crazy emotions. The week after I quit birth control, I had a massage and my massage therapist and Reiki master commented that my body relaxed to a new level. I agreed.

At the time, someone asked me what I was going to do to celebrate such a victory. Victory? Celebrate? I cried those big, uncontrollable tears. The kind of tears where attempting to gracefully wipe them away is pointless. The realization that my reliance on Western medicine and pills had ended took over my emotions. I was scared to believe it was true. My intellect wanted to wait a few months for all the hormones to work out of my system. Only then could I believe my body could not only function, but also remain pain-free without the assistance of medication. It was surreal to let myself consider this a victory. No more medication marked the end of illness, the end of needing something outside of myself to feel well. This question of celebration and victory was the permission I needed to see myself as well. It gave me the strength to break down the remaining barriers so I could fully accept my story and unconditionally love myself.

Part of celebrating has been publicly sharing my experience. Telling my story keeps me in the healing conversation and holds me accountable to the choices that brought me wellness. It's true that we teach what we most need to learn. Being a student and a teacher of this work fulfills me and allows me to grow. Most importantly, as I connect with women and authentically share myself and my story, I feel accepted.

One of the first times after healing that I opened up about living with chronic pain and endometriosis, the words came tumbling out of my mouth. I wasn't scared, holding back, or trying to change the subject. I wasn't trying to move the conversation focus to someone else. The words came from a place of strength deep down in my belly. It felt like time stopped, and the women were listening to me with all their hearts. As I finished what I had to say, I remember thinking that we had spent enough time on me. But question after question kept coming. It was like I was coming alive and being seen for the first time. I felt connected to myself and to these other women who understood me and where I am coming from, thus creating another safe place to explore my true self.

Joy and gratitude have helped me notice when energies are positive and easily flowing. I identified the activities that bring happiness and joy and eliminated those that don't. Considering why an activity feels fun, freeing, joyous, etc. was an important part of discovery. I took notes on everything, journaling constantly. Writing when I could *feel* joy beaming out of me helped me to recognize and identify patterns. I keep a gratitude journal by my bed to reflect not only on what I am grateful for each day, but also on lessons and gifts within struggle. It's a practice of noticing joy, finding hidden gems, and furthering healing, which allow me to breathe happiness into activities as they are happening. Now, when I have an opportunity to authentically connect to other women or share my story, I recognize the whole day as celebrating my talents and expressing myself.

Love. Heal. Celebrate. That is how the journey went for me. Loving and accepting myself as a woman, every part of my body, and my experience gave me strength to release anger for and resentment of the disease. Unconditional love created a space to begin healing my spirit, my mind, and my body. I celebrated successes along my path, and to be honest, at each milestone I thought I was celebrating the end of the journey. In reality, there is no end. Yes, my line in the sand is March 2012, but even as I write this, my journey keeps unfolding. My resilience with shame, negativity, and trauma is far superior to what it used to be, and I know my ability to bounce back will continue to get stronger.

Chronic pain and endometriosis were my demons to conquer. Medical sexual trauma and motherhood were my gremlins to face.

And being true to myself will always be my mountain to climb. As my mask has come off and I evolve into the person I am supposed to be, I am thankful for the lessons chronic pain and endometriosis have taught me. I am living the difference between healing vs. cure, and I wouldn't trade the ups and downs for anything. My journey has led me to being an author, a speaker, and a spiritual growth coach. I share my journey to teach women to listen to their bodies and empower them to heal.

Everyone is worthy and deserving of their own health and well-being. The question is, what are you doing to get there?

CPSIA information can be obtained
at www.ICGtesting.com
Printed in the USA
LVOW12s0133090518
576538LV00001B/80/P